EDITH:

The Cat Who Ate an Elm Tree

by Roz Young
Illustrated by A. Brian Zampier

J. N. TOWNSEND PUBLISHING
EXETER, NEW HAMPSHIRE
1999

Printed in Canada.

Published by:
J. N. Townsend Publishing
12 Greenleaf Drive
Exeter, NH 03833
800-333-9883/603-778-9883
1-880158-23-X

Library of Congress Cataloguing -in-Publication Data
Young, Rosamond McPherson.
Edith : the cat who ate the elm tree / Roz Young.
p. cm.
Includes bibliographical references.
ISBN 1-880158-23-X
1. Young, Rosamond McPherson. 2. Women authors,
American--20th century Biography. 3. Women journalists--
United States Biography. 4. Women cat owners--Ohio--
Dayton Biography. 5. Retirement communities--Ohio--
Dayton. 6. Cats--Ohio--Dayton Anecdotes.
I. Title.

PS3575.085Z465   1999
070'.92--dc21   99-37961
[B]   CIP

Contents

Acknowledgements		vii.
Introduction		xi.
1.	Predicament	1
2.	Edith's Tape	7
3.	A Signal Honor	13
4.	A High Note...	19
5.	...And a Low Note	25
6.	Kidnapped	29
7.	Your Damned Cat	37
8.	Hills and Dales	41
9.	Adirondack Trip	49
10.	Edith, the Blessed	55
11.	Edith and Mrs. Gaskell's Cat	65
12.	Edith, the Thinker	71
13.	Einstein Edith	77
14.	The Hearing Aid Mystery	85
15.	Edith and the New Upholstery	93
16.	Edith and the Bean Juice	99
17.	Elevator Adventure	103
18.	Edith and the Chipmunk	111
19.	The Drinker	117
20.	Pepto Pink	123
21.	A Humbling Lesson	131
22.	Elm Leaf Salad	137
23.	In Appreciation	143
Resources		149

Also by the author:

Two Perfectly Marvellous Cats: A True Story
(paper edition, 1996. J. N. Townsend Publishing)

Acknowledgements

In the pages of this book you will find a number of names which belong to Edith's friends and mine.

Catharine is Catharine Booker, who is responsible for my having Edith in the first place. For this I am eternally grateful to her. Lewis Booker, M. D., was her husband and our family physician. Blackwell, their cat, was Edith's first cat friend.

Freda Stohrer, Ph. D., sings in the choir at Christ Episcopal Church, where Edith would attend if cats were welcome. Freda has a cat named Sarah.

Millie Bingham is a colleague and columnist at the Dayton Daily News. Her cat is named Alice.

Joanne Buck loves gardening and cats. Her cat is Mr. Peabody.

Bill Wild was editor of the editorial page at the newspaper when Edith was kidnapped. He does not have a cat.

Willa is Willa Hedrick, a neighbor before we

moved. Her husband Elvin is a physician and made a house call once when Edith was sick.

Carolyn, who brought Edith the bowl of fish, is Carolyn Young. A woods cat named Marilla has adopted her. Of course Marilla didn't have any name at all until she adopted Carolyn.

Susannah, who gave Edith her video, is Susannah Cowden, who lives down the hall from us at Bethany. She had a cat before she moved here named Miss Ada.

Dorothy, who kept my house clean and in order for many years, is Dorothy Hobbs. She loved Edith, and Edith loved her because she gave Edith a treat every time she came. Dorothy is now retired.

Janis is Janis Sanderson, and she does not have a cat.

Dr. Coatney is Dr. Douglas Coatney, Edith's veterinarian. He has several cats.

Freddie Schaeffer, who knew about the conduit Edith disappeared into, is an acquaintance whose real name is Fredericka.

Dick, who rescued Edith from the Adirondack roof, is Dick Elder and has probably graduated from the university by now and is abroad in the wide, wide world.

What the name of the woman from Chicago who never saw a puffball is, we will never know.

We are grateful to the residents of the Homestead Apartments, who constantly express interest in Edith's doings and her health. We are thankful also to the ducks and geese who tramp past our door, for the good brown mulch where Edith rolls and scratches her back, the sun for shining, and the green grass around our patio. Edith isn't allowed to eat grass any more, but oh, how she would like to!

I hope I haven't forgotten anybody.

Rosamond Young
Dayton, Ohio,
1999

Introduction

When I brought a small brown-orange tabby kitten home from the adoption center one day many years ago, she had been answering to the name of Edna for four months.

This little kitten was going to live in a home of literary pretensions, and it wouldn't do for her to have a non-literary name. Is Edna a literary name?

The Oxford Dictionary of English Christian Names says the etymology of the name Edna is unknown, but it was used several times in the Apocrypha, which is not much of a recommendation, since Protestants, which we both are, consider the Apocrypha uncanonical. The first use of Edna in English literature is in an 1860 novel by C. M. Yonge.

I never heard of C. M. Yonge and doubt whether anybody else in my generation has.

Later I looked C. M. Yonge up in the encyclopedia. She was Charlotte Mary Yonge (1823-1901), a British author who never married and so she had time to write more than one hundred and twenty volumes of novels, manuals, and biographies. Her first novel was in 1853, and considering that she died in 1901, she must have written almost two books a year once she got started. She also worked for thirty years as editor of *The Monthly Packet*, a literary magazine.

Her work was marked by religious feeling and High Church sympathy. She was born in a village called Otterbourne, lived there all her life and died there. Years later I wrote a column for my newspaper about the making of the *Oxford English Dictionary*, reputed by many to be the greatest literary achievement in the history of English letters. Work began on it in 1857; the first edition took seventy years to complete, and supplements are issued every few years to bring the dictionary up to date.

Professor James Murray, original editor of the *OED*, drew from hundreds of brilliant scholars examples of historical uses in literature of the word definitions. One scholar who sent in almost ten thousand citations over a period of twenty years was Dr. William C. Minor. Although he lived only fifty miles from Oxford, he never accepted any of Dr. Murray's invitations to visit the *OED*'s headquarters. Professor Murray, after twenty years, became so curious to about Dr. Minor that he traveled to Crowthorne to see him. When he arrived, he found that Dr. Minor's residence was an insane asylum and that he was a murderer. The two became friends, and Professor Murray often visited Dr. Minor in his pleasant rooms in the asylum.

I looked up in my *OED* in the historical introduction to see if after one hundred years since the first edition Dr. Minor's name was included in the list of contributors. Yes, after more than a century his name is still listed among the contributors before 1884.

The names are listed in alphabetical order. As I started to close the book another name caught my eye. The very last name on the list of contributors is that of Charlotte Mary Yonge.

I knew people would ask me who my cat was named for, and I wanted a name that would not draw blank stares. "My cat is named for a character in a book by Charlotte Mary Yonge" would sink like a stone in the slough of ignorance. A person can write one hundred and twenty books in a lifetime and still not make much of a ripple in the literary pond. With authors it is best seller today and gone tomorrow.

The only literary Edna I could think of offhand was Edna St. Vincent Millay. When I was in college, Edna St. Vincent Millay was all the rage among undergraduates. She wrote volumes of poems, and some of them were good ones. She won a Pulitzer for poetry and lived in New York City, the darling of a group of literary admirers.

In time her poetry went out of fashion, and

she went on the lecture tour to bolster her bank roll. She was nearing the age of fifty when she came to my town to speak to the Dayton English Club, an organization of high-school English teachers. It was during my first year of teaching in Dayton, and I thought, "How wonderful to meet a poet whom I have studied in Modern American Literature." I bought a ticket. The club met in the dining room of one of the downtown department stores and after having tea or coffee and cookies, we anticipated listening to the speaker of the day with relish.

When she appeared, she was pretty much of a shock. The poet had colored her hair with a henna rinse, and she wore a red velvet dress that clashed with her hair. After the introduction by the chairman, she rose to her feet and when the applause had died down, she glared at a microphone that stood in front of the lectern. "I am told," she began, "that I must speak into this...this contraption."

She reached over the lectern and pushed the microphone away.

She picked up a book of her poems and began to read.

"We can't hear you," voices from the back of the room called.

She stopped and glared at the callers.

Just as she was about to resume speaking, a noise like the rushing of wind roared through the room.

"What is that noise?" she asked the chairman.

"It is the air-conditioning system," explained that lady.

"Let it be turned off!" Edna shouted, waving her red-clad arm in a kind of Greek tragic sweep.

The chairman scurried out of the room while St. Vincent, as she always called herself, glared at the club ladies.

The noise abated somewhat, and the chairman resumed her seat.

The poet lifted her book.

The air-conditioning started again.

"I cannot compete with that," she announced, picked up her pocketbook and her book and stalked out of the room.

The chairman and the audience sat stunned, staring at the door through which Miss Millay had disappeared.

After a moment, buzzing among the members broke out. The chairman rose to her feet and grabbed the microphone. "That concludes the program," she said.

Gabbling club members headed for the elevators. The one I squeezed into was packed. One of the women near the back said loudly, "I am going to ask for my money back."

A teacher from my school who was considered literary because she had once written a book stood near the door. She turned around and said,

"Wouldn't you consider it a privilege to pay two dollars to see Shelley throw a fit?"

Most of the woman laughed. Never in her palmiest days did Millay rank with Shelley, but I thought it was a clever remark just the same.

Word went around the club ladies that the poet had too much gin before she showed up at the meeting, and a few years later when we read in the newspapers that she fell down a flight of steps and died of a broken neck, most of the English Club ladies were not surprised.

No, the name of Edna for my cat would simply not do.

I looked over my library shelves for the names of other literary women. Dorothy Parker? Anita Loos? Helen Santmyer? Barbara Tuchman? Jane Austen? P. D. James? Katharine White? Edith Wharton?

Edith Wharton. How about Edith? I looked up Edith in the dictionary of English names. It is an old name, having been popular in England since before 1066. There are many literary Ediths — Edith Wharton, Edith Somerville, Edith Sitwell, Edith Hamilton, to mention four. Then there is Edith with golden hair, who was the sister of Longfellow's laughing Allegra and grave Alice.

I also had a friend named Edith. She and I had exchanged Christmas gifts since the days when you could buy a nice present for two dollars. Over the years the price went up to five dollars, ten dollars, and even twenty-five dollars. Finally we arrived at the stage of life when we didn't need any more things or the bother of thinking up gifts and wrapping them, so finally she gave me a fifty-dollar bill for Christmas and I gave her a fifty-dollar bill. The afternoon I went to the pet adoption center and came home with a kitten, I had Edith's fifty-dollar bill in my pocketbook. I used it to pay the fees for Edna and buy her a few supplies.

Edith would be a better name for my cat than Edna, and besides, she wouldn't even have to change her first initial.

I picked her up and looked into her gold-and-green eyes. "From now on your name is Edith," I told her and made a mark on her forehead with my finger the way the rector does at church. I put her down, went into the kitchen and took a cat treat from a jar. "Edith!" I called.

Edith came running, tail a periscope in the air and a questioning look on her face.

I gave her the treat.

From that moment on, she knew her name.

We lived happily together for six years and then something happened, which is what this book is about.

EDITH:
The Cat Who Ate
an Elm Tree

Actually Edith didn't need therapy yet.

1.

Predicament

Edith was probably headed for trouble.

Edith, my brown-orange tabby with the fawn-colored toes, was six years old. Nothing had ever gone wrong in her life. She had had a few desperate adventures, as you will discover, but they all turned out all right in the end. She lived in a beautiful house on top of a hill surrounded by forty trees, scores of flowering shrubs — forsythia, viburnum, rhododendron — stone walls for climbing, and a fountain for drinking.

Now she was going to lose it.

Somebody was going to make her move into a tiny little two-bedroom apartment in a retirement village. Instead of being a free-roaming cat in woods that she loved, she would have to live indoors all the time. If she went outdoors, she would have to walk on a leash.

Now if you live long enough, you are bound to get old. If you live longer than that, you may become the last leaf on your family tree. If you are the last leaf on your family tree and live in a house on a hill surrounded by forty trees, you could fall down and break something and nobody would find you until much too late.

A person in such a predicament needs to move somewhere that help comes when you push a button. That is why Edith was moving to a retirement home even though at six she was much too young to retire. I wasn't really completely retired, either, from my job as a newspaper columnist, but I could write a column in the new apartment as well as in the big house on the hill, and so I thought we'd better move.

The entire retirement apartment would fit into our living room in the house on the hill and have some space left over. The apartment did, however, have windows on a lake with ducks and geese swimming in it, a garden, and a patio for sunning. I hoped it would appeal to Edith.

Like most cats, Edith does not take any kind of change well. She wants everything to stay the same as it always was.

I worried how she react to moving to a strange (to her), smaller place.

I consulted friends who had cats.

I talked with the head of the adoption center where I found Edith.

I called the president of the Greater Dayton Humane Society. I asked Edith's vet, Dr. Douglas Coatney.

I did not get much useful advice.

A woman from my church said, "I read a story about a cat psychologist in New York City. I think she makes house calls and also consults by mail. I'll see if I can find the article."

She found the article in a Chicago newspaper and sent it. The cat psychologist was Carole C. Wilbourn, and she does make house calls in homes where cats have problems and consults by mail.

We live in Dayton, Ohio, which is rather far from New York City, where Carole Wilbourn lives. I am of the ounce-of-prevention persuasion and wanted advice on how to effect the move so that Edith would make the move comfortably. In my letter I wrote to her,

"Two events are looming up in my six-year-old cat Edith's life. Because we are moving, she has to become an indoor cat and walk on a harness when she goes outside. That will be traumatic for her because she is used to roaming free in our wooded neighborhood. Second, we are moving from a large home to a tiny apartment, and I fear Edith will go into a tizzy: two years ago when we had new carpet and new furniture, she sulked in the kitchen for two months.

"Would you advise keeping her indoors now before we move three months from now, or shall I wait and do it all at once?"

Carole Wilbourn sent a prompt and helpful reply.

"Dear Mrs. Young:

"Continue Edith's life style until you move in September.

"Your positive feelings about your move will affect her well being. Cats are very much affected by peoples' actions, body language and tone of voice. Edith is not yet a senior cat (ten years), but she is not a kitten so she's a tad less flexible.

"In order to provide relaxation techniques and ease her culture shock, I suggest you make an audio tape for her and play it for her frequently before the move, en route on moving day, and after your arrival. Keep reminding Edith that she is adventurous, happy, healthy, safe, and loved. I also suggest that you get a floor-to-ceiling tree for the apartment because of Edith's curtailed exercise opportunities, put brewer's yeast in her food, and practice walking her on a leash."

For the tape she suggested a little talk, using Edith's name frequently, speaking about the good times we have had, reciting a poem, singing a song but above all using her name often. "The sound of its name makes a cat feel very important," said Carole. She sent a present of catnip and some brewer's yeast to put in her food.

I ordered the floor-to-ceiling tree and had it sent to the new apartment. Then I went to work writing out a script for her tape. It took about a week for me to record the tape and have it ready to play for Edith.

2.

Edith's Tape

The tape started with a recording of "Sheep May Safely Graze" by J. S. Bach, who is Edith's favorite composer.

I think he is, anyhow. She never said he wasn't.

Then on the tape the script said, "Edith, we are going to move to a lovely apartment, Edith, on a lake with ducks swimming in the water, Edith. Edith, you are going to be a happy cat in the new apartment, Edith. We will both of us, Edith, love our new house."

The script sounds like the writing of a simpleton, but I noticed when I played it for Edith, the tip of her tail twisted up off the floor and thumped down every time she heard her name.

I remodeled a cat poem by Eleanor Farjeon and read it into the microphone. Here's how it went:

Edith sleeps
Anywhere.
Any table,
Any chair.
Ironing board,
Harpsichord.
Window edge,
In the middle,
On the edge,
On my shoe,
My lap will do,
Fitted in a
Cardboard box,
In the closet
With my socks.
Edith doesn't care
Edith sleeps
Everywhere.

I don't keep my socks in my closet, but the word
Eleanor Farjeon used was "frocks," an old-fashioned
word which does not describe my clothes, chiefly
blazers and skirts. I do have a few dresses, but it
sounds nineteenth century to call them frocks. So I
made it socks. Do not think, however, that I put in
"harpsichord" because it would rhyme with "ironing board." I really did have a harpsichord, and Edith
often slept on it. I sold it when we moved to the

apartment because I thought I wouldn't have room for it. Some of the residents and I were talking one night at dinner about musical instruments shortly after we moved to the retirement village and I remarked regretfully, "Before I moved here I had a harpsichord."

Quicker than I can type this, one of the men at the table piped up, "I hope you called the doctor."

Next came a song. I am not a good singer, having never had lessons, but I am vigorous, and I can keep the melody without going flat. For the words I rewrote a William Shakespeare song from *Two Gentlemen of Verona*. Schubert set the song to music, and I sang it lustily a capella into the microphone. Sing along if you know the melody, and if nobody else is home.

> Who is Edith?
> What is she,
> That everyone commends her?
> Holy, fair, and wise is she,
> The heavens such beauty lend her
> That admired she might be.
> That admired she might be.
>
> Is Edith kind as she is fair?
> For beauty dwells with kindness.

Love does to her eyes repair
To help him of his blindness
And being helped,
Inhabits there.
And being helped,
Inhabits there.

Then to Edith us let us sing
That Edith is excelling.
She excels each noble thing
Upon this dull earth dwelling,
Let us garlands to her bring,
Let us garlands to her bring.

"This is the end of your tape, Edith," I said into the microphone. "Edith is the most beautiful cat in the world. Edith is a patient, devoted, under-standing, trusting, polite cat. There is no cat like Edith. Everybody who knows Edith loves her.

"Matchless Edith. Intelligent Edith. Lovable Edith. Cat of cats, Edith.

"Who is the cat of cats?"

"Edith is the cat of cats."

I flipped on the record player and a reprise of "Sheep May Safely Graze" filled the room.

I played the tape every day for the three months it took us to get ready to move. I programmed it to play whenever I left Edith alone in the house.

One day a visiting friend stayed in the house

while I went to work. I forgot to tell him about the tape.

When I came home, he whistled a couple of bars from "Who is Edith, what is she?"

"Oh, dear," I said. "I forgot."

"Edith went under the bed while the tape was playing," he said. "I didn't think it was that bad."

3.

A Signal Honor

Twice before moving day, I took Edith out to
see the new apartment. The first time she stalked
from room to room, yowling in top voice. She didn't
like this place, not one little bit. When I took her
out on the patio on her leash to see the lovely lake
and the ducks, she pulled out of the leash and headed
for home, five miles away. I had a hard time catching her.

The second trip she checked out all the rooms
again, looked at me as if to say, "I've been here before," and when I opened a kitchen drawer to show
it to her, she hopped in and took a nap.

She spent Wednesday, the day we moved, at
Catharine's house, playing with Blackwell. When I
took her to the apartment after the moving people
left, she walked right in as if she knew she lived there.

For the next two days she sat around watching

while I unpacked boxes and found places to put our belongings.

On Saturday morning after breakfast I had to go downtown to get my hair done. I looked for Edith to tell her I would be back shortly.

I couldn't find her to tell her anything.

She wasn't in the kitchen.

She wasn't in the bedroom.

She wasn't in the office.

She wasn't in either bathroom.

I finally had to leave.

As soon as I returned two hours later, I hunted for her.

She wasn't under the bed.

She wasn't in the closets.

She wasn't under the bureau.

She wasn't under the dresser.

She wasn't on top of any of the cupboards.

She wasn't anywhere.

Where could she be? I began to feel panicky. Had she escaped outdoors somehow and was on her way home? Had she slipped into the hall and was even now loose in a building with three floors and sixty-eight apartments?

I stood in our foyer, which is about the size of a card table, and thought.

Was there anywhere else in the apartment where she could be? "Edith! Edith! Where are you?" I called.

"Meow."

She was there somewhere!

I looked around.

There was one place I hadn't looked. Behind a pair of doors in the foyer in a space forty inches wide and twenty deep is a washing machine with a dryer on top of it. I opened the doors.

There stood Edith, her head wedged between the washer and the wall. She looked up at me, a pitiable expression on her face.

"Why, Edith," I said, "how long have you been in this dark hole? Come on out."

She couldn't come out. She was stuck. Evidently she had walked into the opening on the other side when I opened the door, crawled around the washer and kept going until she could go no further. "You will have to back up, Edith," I told her. "Turn around and go out the way you came in."

Edith couldn't turn around. There isn't room for anything between the washer and the wall except a coat of paint.

I tried to push her backwards. I couldn't budge her. She was too fat.

"Edith, you are just like Winnie the Pooh when he went to visit Rabbit and ate too much. Do you know what happened? He got stuck in the door and couldn't get through and he was wedged in too far to back out. You know what he had to do? He had to stay there until he got thin enough to get through Rabbit's door. Now how am I going to get you out of this place? You can't stay there until you get thin like Pooh."

I would have to call the maintenance department to move the washer, but it was Saturday and I didn't know whether anybody worked on Saturday. Besides, this was the first time I had lived in a place not my own, and I didn't want to start making requests only three days after we had moved in.

I draped myself over the washer and grabbed her by the fur of her back and heaved. It must have hurt to be yanked upward by fur and skin alone, but she didn't complain at all. Up she came.

Once released from that Stygian cave, she hurried to the kitchen to replenish her calories.

Edith made the adjustment to her new home faster and better than I thought she would. The scales at our old house were in the kitchen by her food bowls, and she used to sit on it for me to see whether she had gained weight and have a little something to eat if she hadn't. In our new home the scales are in her bathroom, where I never go except to clean her litter box behind the shower curtain. One day I found Edith sitting on the scales in the bathroom all by herself.

Just after we moved I took her to Dr. Douglas Coatney for her monthly checkup. He cleans her teeth, which involves holding her head with one hand while he pries the tartar loose with a steel instrument. Then he weighs her.

Last he clips her claws. He turns her on her side to do this and has one of the office staff hold her. She doesn't like having her claws clipped, and we all talk soothingly to her during the procedure and caution her not to growl. "One foot done already, Edith. Now another one. No, no, no. No growling, or Dr. Coatney will feel bad and that makes him nervous. There. Only two to go."

Edith looks at me with her great, big green eyes and seems to ask, "Why do you let him do this to me?"

When Dr. Coatney finished Edith's last claw on this particular day, he said, "Edith, you did very well. You growled only once today."

While he talked to her, he stroked her back, and she lay quietly on the table. Then he leaned over and right on the top of her beautiful brown and fawn head with the black stripes, he planted a great big kiss.

I wrote in my newspaper column a few days later about the signal honor Edith received from Dr. Coatney. The next time we went to his office, he said, "Since your column was in the paper, I have had to kiss all the other dogs and cats who come into the office."

...a veteran parade rider

4.
A High Note...

The first week we moved into our new home Edith received an invitation from the Humane Society of Greater Dayton. The society had been formed one hundred years before by a few prominent Dayton citizens to promote the principles of humane treatment to all creatures. Edith was invited to ride as a Very Important Cat in the society's pet parade.

When I showed her the letter, she didn't say yes and she didn't say no. She scratched her chin on the edge of the letter, and I answered for her that she would be thrilled.

This was to be only the second parade the society had held in its history. The first one was in 1924 when the society opened a new animal shelter. "Hundreds of thousands of people lined the streets," said a newspaper of the day. "Bugles blared,

19

bands marched, floats glided down Main Street as 1,500 entrants with their pets waved at the crowds. Pets ranged from goldfish to goats. There were monkeys, snakes, raccoons, ponies and every kind of cat and dog.

"Judges gave out two hundred prizes. Free ice cream went to all entrants and visitors."

The shelter had lasted for seventy years, but it became overcrowded and the society needed $1 million for a new one. This parade was to mark the kickoff for a campaign to raise the money.

It was scheduled to begin at ten o'clock on a Saturday morning. Edith has an exhibition cage which is all wire sides and top so that she is completely visible when she is in it. I put her in the cage and set her on the front seat of my car. We drove around to pick up my friend Millie, who had volunteered to go along and drive the car to a parking garage while I stayed with Edith on the downtown plaza where the parade was to form.

It was a lovely October day with bright sunshine and balmy air.

When we arrived, entrants were already strolling around the plaza: big dogs, little dogs, dogs dressed in costumes, and one cat on a leash.

A society member drove up to the curb where we were standing. She drove a brand new white convertible with the top down.

"This is Edith's car," she said. I put Edith in her exhibition cage on the folded down top of the convertible, and I perched beside her. Millie rode down inside the car.

One of the society's members drove the car, while two more walked in front carrying a banner that said "Edith" in sparkling letters.

At exactly ten o'clock a high school band began playing as it marched up Fourth Street. One hundred animals and their human companions marched behind the band. The dogs all walked; the one other cat rode in the arms of its owner.

Our convertible swung out into line. We turned the corner onto Main Street. Edith sat straight up in her cage and looked from right to left like a veteran parade rider. I was so proud of her my chest expanded visibly.

As we approached Third and Main, the geographical center of our city, I said to Edith, "You and I have reached the pinnacle of our careers. Here we both are, riding in a convertible down Main Street in our own home town. To how many others has this honor happened? Not very many. Orville and Wilbur Wright once rode down Main Street in a parade, of course. But who else? Nobody I can think of.

"Edith, savor this moment. I am reasonably certain you are the only cat ever to ride as a celebrity in a parade downtown in the city of Dayton. You are a Historic Cat. Hooray for Edith! Hooray for the Humane Society!"

We rolled past the court house, on the steps of which another celebrity named Abraham Lincoln once spoke, continued to Second Street, turned the corner and down Second to Sinclair College for a press conference.

There the president of the society made a speech and announced that the fund drive had already started with an anonymous gift of $250,000. Everybody cheered.

Actually it was the president's husband who had made the anonymous gift, we found out later.

After the press conference, we had some refreshments, and Millie brought the car around and we went back to normal, everyday life.

One disappointment marred the day, but not very much. The downtown area of our city is quite different today from what it was in 1924 when the society held its last parade. During the week the streets are fairly busy with downtown workers coming and going into office buildings and popping into restaurants for lunch. But the shoppers now go to the suburban malls, and hardly anybody at all comes downtown on Saturday morning. While hundreds of thousands lined the curbs for the first parade, somewhat fewer lined them for the second. I did see a man and his wife at the corner of Second Street, and I waved at them, but they didn't wave back. But even if they were the only spectators who came, nothing will ever dim the recollection of that glorious ride down Main Street for Edith and me.

...not a runway cat

5.

... And a Low Note

After the parade the society gave a banquet to raise more money for the new animal shelter. Edith was invited to take part in a Pet Affair. Fifteen Daytonians were invited to bring their pets and promenade with them on a runway for the delight of hundreds of guests at the $50 a plate dinner.

All the other animals invited were dogs of assorted kinds — a Doberman, a poodle, a schnauzer, a dachshund, an English setter. Edith was the only cat.

Dogs are natural born promenaders. With just a little training they will march smartly with a person along a sidewalk, up a country road, or along a runway on a stage.

Cats, however, do not promenade. Edith will go for a walk with me, but she goes where she wants to go, not where I want her to go. Before the dinner I worried that all the dogs would march down the runaway to the applause of the guests, and then I would bring up the rear, trying to shoo or drag Edith along.

At the dinner things started off badly. Edith had to stay in her exhibition cage in the corner of a large room while all the guests banqueted. Other occupants of the room were dogs of many sizes and extensive vocabularies. Some of the dogs barked ceaselessly.

Edith does not like dogs, whether barking or not. She crouched in her cage and cried while the dogs barked.

An L-shaped runway had been constructed in the banquet room. The master of ceremonies was to station himself in the corner of the L. He would interview the pet owner, and then pet and owner were to promenade down the runway.

I had supposed that Edith and I would be last on the runway because people whose last name starts with Y or Z are usually last on every list. But lo, this time, like Abou Ben Adhem, Edith's name led all the rest.

Just before her appearance a society member took Edith out of her cage and tried to put a pink sweater on her. The sweater had a cowl neck and long sleeves. Edith had never had worn clothes before, and she had never seen the volunteer before.

The volunteer pulled one of Edith's front legs

through a sleeve of the sweater, but soon as she tried to put the other front leg through the other sleeve, Edith pulled the first leg out of the first sleeve. The two of them were wrestling when the master of ceremonies called out Edith's name.

The volunteer handed Edith to me with the sweater around Edith's neck. I hoisted her into my arms and carried her through the ranks of yapping dogs to the runway. She squirmed and wiggled and jumped out of my grasp onto the runway. I started down the runway, expecting Edith to follow me as does around the house or outdoors. But the lights and the barking dogs and the laughing guests upset her usual aplomb, and she dived into the understructure of the runway. I grabbed for her and caught hold of her sweater. Edith lunged and disappeared, and I was left in front of several hundred people holding nothing but an empty sweater. The master of ceremonies never did interview us.

I managed to coax Edith out of the under structure of the runway and put her back in her cage. We watched while all the other animals promenaded. Some walked on leashes, and some simply followed their owners. Several performed tricks. One dog walked on his hind legs. Not one of the dogs acted up. I stood by Edith's cage engulfed in embarrassment, and we left the banquet hall a little later in ignominy.

Feline fame aside

Where's Edith?

6.

Kidnapped

Edith never said a word about whether she missed our old neighborhood after we moved, but I certainly did. Often when I drove home from downtown, I went out of my way a few blocks just to drive past our old house and reminisce about the adventures we had there.

One of the most harrowing was the time Edith was kidnapped.

One afternoon a day or so after Christmas one year Edith hopped up on the desk and sat down on my income tax.

I keep a desk chair for Edith right by my own. She tramps all over the desk top, rubbing her chin against the pencil holder and looking for rubber bands.

This time she snoozed for about an hour on my tax form, woke up, stretched and headed for the kitchen. In a moment I heard her name tag clicking against the food dish. Then she appeared at my side, a question in her eyes.

"Show me what you want, Edith."

She walked out of the office, looking over her back now and then to be sure I was following. She led me to the front door. She paused on the threshold, considering whether she really wanted to go out. She stepped onto the porch. "Don't stay out too long," I cautioned. "It's cold today."

By dinner time the dark had begun to creep down the hill. I went to the door, expecting Edith to be waiting outside. But she had not come home yet.

I prepared my dinner and sat by the window eating, expecting her to hop up on the window sill any moment, but she did not appear.

She did not return all evening long. The temperature on the thermometer sank to zero. Where was that cat?

I waited up until midnight. Finally I went to bed, but I could not sleep. Every hour I went to the front door, turned on the porch light, opened the door and called her. She never came bounding up on the porch.

She was not on the front porch in the morning. Edith had never before stayed out all night. Maybe she had been hit by a car. Perhaps she was locked in a garage somewhere. I had heard about a cat in the neighborhood who had been accidentally locked in a garage for two weeks while the garage owners were in Florida.

I called the newspaper an put and ad in the lost and found department.

I called the adoption center where I got Edith. Edith's picture and registration number are on file there. She wears the number on her collar. A recorded voice said that the center was closed until after New Year's Day and for help to call the Humane Society.

I called the society. "My cat is missing," I told the woman who answered. I gave her my name.

There was a pause.

"You don't mean Edith?"

"Yes. Edith."

"Good heavens, I read about her in the paper all the time. Tell me what she looks like. I'll go see if we have a cat that answers her description."

After I described Edith, she left the telephone. When she came back, she said, "No, Edith has not been brought in. I will put a note on the bulletin board for staff members to be on the lookout for her. I suggest you call the street department, too."

I called.

"You don't mean Edith!" said the street department lady.

"Yes."

"Oh, dear, that's too bad. I will get word to the drivers. If they pick her up, I will call you."

A fist closed around my heart. What shape would she be in if they picked her up? Dead, no doubt.

I called my neighbors to look in their garages.

I called the Oakwood police in case Edith had gone to visit Blackwell.

I called Catharine.

I washed up Edith's dishes and put the on the counter. What else could I do?

I called Bill Wild, my editor at the newspaper. "Do you suppose you could put a little note on the Op-Ed page about Edith being missing?" I asked him. "Maybe run her picture? There is one in the files in the reference library."

He said he would consider it.

They day wore on. Nobody called. Edith did not return. I wept. I read poetry about cats who had died. Oh, I was a tragic figure, I tell you.

She was not there again the next morning. I turned to the Op-Ed page, half hoping. The Op-Ed page is where my column always appeared before I retired. Now it is there on Saturday mornings only.

There was nothing about Edith on the page. I felt chagrined. I really shouldn't have asked.

Then I looked on the editorial page.

There was Edith's picture. Under it was this editorial:

Feline Fame aside, where's Edith?

Edith is making the news again by disappearing from Roz's northwest Kettering home, little ingrate.

The search has disclosed so far that Edith is as well or better known than Roz is to the police and street department personnel, at any rate.

Edith, wherever you are, please call 293-9722 or 225-2380 today, and be ready for a good talking to.

I sat there at the breakfast table, looking at Edith's picture and thinking what a wonderful thing Bill Wild had done.

The telephone rang. I jumped.

"You don't know me," a man's voice said. "I have just been reading the newspaper over breakfast, and I have your cat. If you will tell me where you live, I will bring her to you."

I thought Wordsworth had a peculiar problem when his heart leaped up when he beheld a rainbow in the sky.

I was wrong about Wordsworth. Hearts do leap sometimes. Mine did then.

I gave him the directions and ran to get dressed.

After a while a black car appeared in the driveway.

33

A tall man in a brown parka hurried up the steps. He had Edith in his arms. I swung the door open. "Oh, do please come in," I said.

"No, I can't. I am on my way to work."

"But how did you happen to find Edith?"

He told me. "Please," I said, "I want to give you a reward. Please come inside out of the cold."

He shook his head no. He turned and disappeared down the steps.

I picked up Edith and danced all through the living room for pure joy. Oh, frabjous day.

I filled her food and water bowls.

I canceled the ad in the newspaper and called everybody I had reported Edith's disappearance to.

Two days later another editorial appeared in our newspaper.

Happy New Year: It's the Cat's Meow

Truth is stranger than fiction, as Lord Byron wrote.

We'll get to that in a moment.

The first truth is there was some skepticism on the editorial board about running the snippet on Roz Young's lost cat, Edith. Tuesday morning. It was fortunate — and absurdly good luck — that the wisdom of heart prevailed over the logic of head. A reader saw the editorial and Edith's picture. His small daughter had recently brought in a stray cat, said to be collarless. A little detective work turned up Edith"'s collar in the little girl's bureau drawer, and a bit of a cat-napping tale. He called Roz. Now cat, collar and owner are happily reunited.

Count on Roz writing about it in a week or two. But she didn't get the name of her bene-factor or the now catless child. Some veteran reporter she is.

Anyway, it's a nice way to start off the New Year.

I thank whatever gods may be that the father of the little girl is the kind of person who reads the editorials.

Otherwise I probably would never have seen Edith again.

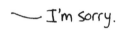

7.

Your Damned Cat

It was September when Edith and I moved into Bethany. On the patio outside our living room door stood a table, four chairs and an umbrella. Otherwise, there was nothing.

I sallied out to the garden store and bought a number of pots, several bags of potting soil and a few chrysanthemums to plant in the pots. They did make the patio look pretty.

As winter approached, I wondered what to do with them. It would be a shame to leave them in the pots, which would be the end of them. I called the grounds supervisor to ask if there was a place on the demesne where he could plant the chrysanthemums.

He came around to see me and suggested, "You could plant them in the ground right around your patio."

The garden around the patio had already been

planted by the grounds department with dwarf spirea, holly, and euonymous. It never occurred to me that I could add to or subtract anything from the institutional planting. When I learned I could, I was delighted. Digging in the good, brown earth is one of my favorite activities, and coming home from the nursery with a flat of flowers to plant is a happy occasion.

The ground around the patio is not good and brown but is blue-gray clay so stiff you could make pottery out of it. I called in a nursery and contracted to have much of the clay soil hauled away and replaced with several truckloads of earth from a company that calls itself the Garden of Eden.

Of course, before I moved from our old house, I sold all my garden tools — shovels, sprayers, spades, trowels, hoes, plant cages, garden cart and wagon and a wheel barrow. Here I was with a garden to plant but without a tool to my name.

Joanne is a friend who likes nothing better than stopping at nurseries or garden centers when we go out to lunch. One afternoon we went to a garden store and had a great time buying a trowel, a spade, a rake, a garden cart, gloves and a few other oddments I would need for working in the soil and planting the chrysanthemums.

When we were about to get into the car and leave, another car drove up beside us and parked. Out of it stepped a man and a woman. They greeted

Joanne, and she introduced me to them, explaining that they were friends of hers who lived in a cottage at Bethany. I was about to extend my hand when the man, a gray-haired chap with a scowling face, exclaimed, "You! You and your damned cat have ruined Bethany!"

Such a silence you never heard.

I stood staring at him. I couldn't believe I had heard him right, but his voice was as loud as a chorus of ten. Nobody in my whole life had ever spoken to me like that. The phrase "your damned cat" kept reverberating in my mind, and I thought fleetingly about slapping him in the face.

Grown-ups don't slap people, at least where I live. I would like to have made some cutting remark that would devastate him, but at moments like those I can't think of a thing to say. I stood there, levelling blue-eyed shafts from my eyes that I hoped would strike him like thunderbolts. Then I said, "Come on, Joanne, Let's go."

I jerked open the car door, jumped inside and slammed the door shut louder than was necessary.

We drove away.

"Why would anybody say a thing like that?" I asked Joanne.

"Oh, he is that way," she explained. "He probably thought he was being funny."

"I do not think it was funny."

"That was evident."

I learned later that some of the cottage residents had complained to the administration about allowing cats on the campus because they did not want them strolling through their yards, catching their birds and using their flower beds for litter boxes. He was probably one of those.

Some time later Edith and I were invited to a book store near our house to autograph copies of a book I had previously written about her. Edith lay on a soft rug and let people pet her. I made a speech and then sat at a desk to sign books.

We were there for several hours. A man and woman who had been standing in line for a long time came up to the desk. The woman handed me a book to sign. I looked at her and then at him. They were Joanne's friends from the parking lot.

At once I felt the fur rising along my backbone. I wanted to say, "This is my damned cat," but wisdom prevailed, I signed the book, handed it to her and thanked her for coming.

The man looked at me across the desk and said, "I'm sorry." He hurried away.

I never saw him again. I would have liked to say, "Edith and I accept your apology," but I did not have the chance.

I wonder if his wife made him say he was sorry, or was it his own idea.

8.

Hills and Dales

For a while after we moved to the new apartment, whenever Edith saw me get out her harness, she hid under the bed. When I lured her out with a treat and tried to put it on her, she fought with her claws and little nips of her sharper-than-a-serpent's teeth.

After a time, however, she learned that the harness meant a walk in the park or the cemetery. Now she stands still while I slip the loop over her head and lies on her side while I fasten the strap behind her front legs. Then she hurries into the carrying case.

One warm Saturday afternoon Catharine and I thought it would be fun for Edith to go for an unrestricted walk through our old neighborhood. We used to live on the edge of a large park called Hills and Dales, and often when Edith was a free roaming cat, she explored the wooded pathways. The park covers hundreds of acres with little paths striking off in many directions.

We parked the car at the entrance to the park and let Edith go where she liked without a leash. The road winds up a steep, pathway to the statue of John H. Patterson astride his horse Skinner, sitting on top of the hill and overlooking the park. Mr. Patterson is the one who gave the park to the city.

Up the pathway Edith started, going uphill all the way. Trudging along as if she knew where she was going. Little paths diverged off into the park, but Edith kept straight on until she came to the statue. Catharine and I followed close behind. By the time she reached the top of the hill Edith's little red tongue was hanging out and she seemed to be breathing through her mouth.

"I think she is tired," I said. "It's a long way back to the car. I'll walk down the road to pick up the car and drive up the hill. You start downhill with Edith, and I'll pick you up when we meet. We'd better put the leash on her because she might dash out into traffic."

Edith stood perfectly still while I put on her leash and handed the end of it to Catharine. I set off down the hill at a faster pace than Catharine could walk with Edith. On long walks Edith sits down a lot.

I drove the car up the winding roadway, expecting to meet Catharine and Edith at every turn, but they were not to be seen. At last when I rounded one curve near the middle of the hill, I saw Catharine sitting in a ditch by the side of the road, her head sort of sunk on her chest. I parked the car and jumped out. "What's the matter? Did you have an accident?" I thought maybe she had turned an ankle.

She held up the empty harness.

"Where is Edith?"

"Two cars came along the road and frightened her," Catharine explained. "She jumped down into the ditch and ran into this pipe here." She indicated the open end of a conduit. "When I pulled on the harness, she must have turned around and backed out of it. Anyhow, she has disappeared."

I jumped down into the ditch.

There in front of us yawned a large pipe issuing out of the ground. I tried to look into it. You have heard of the Black Hole of Calcutta, no doubt. I knelt down and called into the hole. Nothing but silence rolled back at me. Right away a horrible picture flashed into my mind.

When I was a girl, the nation was transfixed over what happened to Floyd Collins. Floyd, a thirty-year-old Kentuckian, went exploring in an underground passage near Mammoth Cave. A boulder slipped, fell across his ankle and trapped him in a narrow passage 126 feet under the surface. A neighbor boy heard his calls a day later and ran for help. Help came, and 150 reporters from newspapers all over the country turned up at the scene.

William Miller, a reporter from the Louisville Courier Journal, made five trips into the dark tunnel to talk to Collins and to try to help him. On one of the trips he took an electric wire and light bulb, which illuminated the area where Collins lay, and took a photo of him which appeared on the front pages of newspapers all over the country. Miller and the brother of Floyd Collins fastened a harness around him and tried to pull him free. But a six-ton rock on his foot could not be moved.

Efforts to drill into the side of a hill and tunnel through to Collins had to be abandoned because of fears that the rocks would shift and crush him to death. He lay in his underground tomb for twenty-eight days, while all the world stood still, waiting for the inevitable news that he had died of exposure.

I was twelve years old when Floyd Collins was trapped underground, and I never forgot that awful scene.

Peering into the black hole, I saw the portrait of the dead Floyd Collins in my mind as if it were yesterday. "Edith!" I called. "Edith! Edith! Edith!"

What was I going to do? In my mind I could picture Edith creeping through the sewer system under Hills and Dales park. No telling how many miles the sewer stretched.

"Edith! Edith! Edith!"

Freddie, a woman from the neighborhood, whom we both knew, came walking along the road. "What are you doing in the ditch?" she asked. "Is something wrong?"

"Oh, yes. Edith has disappeared into this sewer here. No telling how many miles it stretches through the park. What ever I going to do?"

"Edith? You mean Edith who used to live down on Springhill? You mean Edith that I read about in the paper? Edith?"

"Yes."

"Well, this pipe isn't part of the sewer system," she said. "It is a conduit that runs under the road which goes back into the park. The other end of the conduit is about 100 yards up the hill."

I ran up the hill to the other end. Down into the ditch I ran and stuck my head into the black hole. "Edith!" I called. "Edith! Come out. Edith!"

There was nothing but silence.

Freddie joined me in the ditch. "Call her again."

"Edith! Edith!"

"I hear her," said Freddie. "She answers every time you call." My ears are no good, and I couldn't hear her at all.

"Keep calling," said Freddie. "I'll go down to the other end and tell Catharine to call."

I sat in the ditch trying to think what to do. At last I saw Edith coming toward me out of the blackness. She came almost with reaching distance and then a car came along and scared her, and she disappeared once more into the hole.

I eyed the conduit. It was about eighteen inches in diameter. I didn't know whether a woman of my size could crawl on her stomach and wriggle through the conduit and chase her out the other end. There was water in the pipe and might be snakes and stones and heaven knows what else, but I would do anything for Edith.

"I am going in after her," I shouted to Freddie's disappearing back. "If I get stuck, call the fire department." She waved and went on.

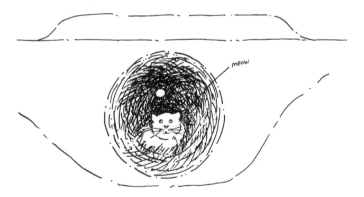

I decided to go head first and had squeezed myself in about up to my waist when at the other end Catharine gave a loud shout. I backed out of the conduit and sat up. Freddie came running. "Edith came out!" she shouted. "Catharine caught her."

"I'll get the carrying case out of the car," I called to Freddie.

By the time I got to my feet and started down the hill, Freddie had already brought the case out of the car, and when Edith saw it, she absolutely bolted to get into it.

Edith didn't say one word all the way home, and when we got into the apartment, she flopped down on the floor in the kitchen and went to sleep. I was so exhausted from the ordeal that I did, too.

On the sofa, not the kitchen floor.

9.
Adirondack Trip

The Hills and Dales conduit is just up the street from the Adirondack Terrace Apartments. I go past it every time I drive home from town, and I think about the horrible ordeal when Edith was marooned there for three days and nights.

Edith didn't come home from her breakfast check of the neighborhood one day. She didn't come that night, either.

I put an ad in the Lost and Found. I called the street departments of three suburbs. I showed her picture to the mail man. I tramped through the neighborhood, calling.

Maybe she has been kidnapped again," said Catharine. "Have you checked the attic?"

"I have." Edith disappeared into the attic a whole day once.

"I will come over after lunch."

When she came, we walked through all the back yards for blocks around. We peered into garages, looked under porches, and checked wood piles. Edith wasn't anywhere.

We finally went back home.

As we turned into the driveway, Catharine said, "We didn't go up Willowgrove." My house was on the corner of Springhill and Willowgrove. Edith liked to take naps right in the middle of Willowgrove.

"I walked up that way yesterday."

"Let's walk up there again. You know she thinks it is her own private street. And you know how bad your hearing is."

We set off up the hill, calling. As we passed the second house from the corner Catharine stopped. "I hear a cat!" she exclaimed.

She called again. "Do you hear her?"

"No."

"Edith! There. She answered. Did you hear her?"

"No."

"She is somewhere around here. I recognize her voice."

We walked on, with Catharine calling. She turned off into the back yard of the Adirondack Terrace Apartments. "Look in the bushes," she said.

"Edith!"

"Meow." I heard her that time.

"Look up," said Catharine.

Peering over the roof edge of the apartment house three stories above us was Edith. The apartment has a hip roof, and she had to brace herself to look over the edge.

"How in the world did she ever get up there?"

Catharine pointed to a tall tree next to the apartment. "Probably climbed up there and jumped. But with the wind the way it is switching the branches around, she couldn't jump back."

"How will we ever get her down?"

"Maybe you could stand on the window sill of that window directly under Edith and reach up and grab her."

I am not much for standing on window sills three stories up, but I would do anything for Edith.

We walked into the apartment building and up three flights of stairs. I knocked on the door of the one I figured was under Edith.

A young man answered the door.

"My cat is on the roof directly over your apartment," I said. "She is right above one of your windows. May we come in?"

"I can get on the roof," he said. "I have a key. There's a place up there for sunbathing. Wait till I get my shoes on."

In a moment he joined us, key in hand. "I am home from the university, working on a paper," he explained. "My name is Dick."

We told him our names. He walked down a half flight of stairs and unlocked a door. A ladder was mounted against the wall inside the doorway. Up the ladder he climbed, some twenty feet. He disappeared through a trap door. Above the door we could see the sky. Dick's face appeared against the sky. "What's your cat's name?" he asked.

"Edith."

He disappeared.

After a while his head appeared in the opening. "She comes close to me," he said, "but when I reach for her, she backs away."

"She'll come to me," said Catharine. She took off her jacket and handed it to me. Up the ladder she went.

"Wow, this is terrible," she called back when she reached the top. "There isn't anything to grab on to."

I saw a hand reach through the opening, and Catharine disappeared.

Then Dick backed down the ladder. "She came right to your friend," he said. "I will get a knapsack, strap it on and put her in it."

He came back with the knapsack and disappeared up the ladder.

In a little while he stuck his head through the opening. "She won't stay in the knapsack."

I thought a moment. Then the solution came to me. "Get a pillowcase, tie her in it and put the pillowcase in the knapsack."

He came down again and fetched a pillowcase from his apartment.

After a while he started backing down the ladder with Edith yowling with the strength of ten from the pillowcase.

He handed me the knapsack. I opened the pillowcase enough for her to get her head through. When she saw me, I swear a look of relief came over her face. She stopped howling.

Dick came down.

"I can't get down," Catharine yelled from the top of the ladder.

Dick went back up the ladder. "Turn over on your stomach and ease your legs through the opening," he directed.

"There isn't anything to hold on to!"

"I will guide your feet to the top rung of the ladder," said Dick. "After you get your feet on it, you will be all right."

Catharine stuck her feet through the opening, and Dick grabbed her legs and eased her feet to the ladder. With help from him on every step, she made it safely down. "I will never go up there again," she said when she was down. "Why, it must be twenty feet to the concrete floor. I could have cracked my skull or broken a leg. The next time your cat goes up on the roof, it's up to you to get her down. You'll have to call the fire department or some animal rescue league."

"There won't be a next time," I said. "Edith never makes the same mistake twice."

She never did, either.

Dick wouldn't take a money reward. But he would take a bottle of whiskey I found in my liquor cabinet.

10.

Edith, the Blessed

Cats have won a place in the hearts of men and women, boys and girls of all races, all religions and those with no religion at all. Cats don't trouble their minds about religion. Unlike us, they don't know that life will end one day. Their heaven is right here and now with their loving owners.

Anglicans, however, Roman Catholics, Episcopalians, and United Methodists have a rite called the Blessing of the Animals.

One day I read in the newspaper that there was to be a Blessing of the Animals at the United Theological Seminary on Saturday afternoon. Why not have Edith blessed, I thought.

I put her into her carrying case and set off with her in the car for a long trip across our city.

Edith does not like going in her carrying case anywhere. It is small and confining, and she can't see out of it very well. Usually to her mind the carrying case means a trip to the vet to have her nails clipped and her teeth cleaned.

Her only way to show her displeasure when she is in the case is to yowl. And yowl she did on this sunny afternoon, all the way downtown, across the bridge and up an avenue to the campus of the seminary.

The campus is a large grassy square with number of trees and buildings around it.

Chairs had been set up on the grass and a small stage built. Dotted here and there sat or lay large numbers of dogs, many cats, a boa constrictor, a cage of hamsters and one pony. All were resting on the grass beside their owners, who sat on folding chairs.

I opened Edith's carrier and snapped her leash around her neck as she stepped out on the grass. She explored the area around my chair for a little while, but she showed no interest in meeting any of the other animals. The dogs were well behaved, none of them barking.

Edith sat up on her haunches beside my chair, ears perked forward, turning her head this way and that, sampling the air.

At the announced time, a young man sat down by the side of the stage at a keyboard that had been set up on the grass. The president of the seminary, a pastor from the First Lutheran Church, the president of the Humane Society of Greater Dayton, a University of Dayton professor, and the secretary of SICSA, the pet adoption center where I found Edith, marched in procession onto the stage and sat down facing the audience.

The president of the seminary stood, dressed in a black robe with the school colors, red and gold, on his hood, said, "The service today follows the Roman Catholic Order for the Blessing of Animals. Responses for the audience are printed in the program in italics.

"The service will begin with the singing of a hymn, the words of which were written by St. Francis of Assisi, patron saint of all animals."

The organist began playing and we sang:

> All creatures of our God and King,
> Lift up your voices, let us sing:
> Alleluia, alleluia!
> Bright burning sun with golden beams,
> Pale silver moon that gently gleams,
>
> O praise him, O praise him, alleluia,
> Alleluia, alleluia, alleluia.
> Great rushing winds and breezes soft,
> You clouds that ride the heavens aloft,
> O praise him, Alleluia!
> Fair rising morn, with praise rejoice,

Stars nightly shining, find a voice,

Swift flowing water, pure and clear,
make music for your lord to hear,
Alleluia, alleluia!
Fire, so intense and fiercely bright,
you give to us both warmth and light,

Dear mother earth, you day by day
Unfold your blessing on our way,
O praise him, alleluia!
All flowers and fruits that in you grow,
Let them his glory also show:

All you with mercy in your heart,
forgiving others, take your part,
O sing now, Alleluia!
All you that pain and sorrow bear,
praise God, and on him cast your care:

And even you, most gentle death,
Waiting to hush our final breath,
O praise him, Alleluia!
You lead back home the child of God,
for Christ, our Lord, that way has trod:

Let all things their creator bless,
and worship him in humbleness,
O praise him, Alleluia!
Praise God the Father, praise the Son,
and praise the Spirit, three in one.

When the sound of the hymn faded into silence, the representative of the Society for the Preservation of Stray Animals, a short, pillowy woman with red hair, rose.

"A reading from Genesis, 1; verses 20 to 28." she said.

In the beginning when God created the heavens and the earth, God said, `Let the waters team with abundance of living creatures, and on earth let birds fly beneath the dome of the sky.' And so it happened: God created the great sea monsters and all kinds of swimming creatures with which the water teems, and all kinds of winged birds. God saw how good it was and God blessed them, saying, `Be fertile, multiply, and fill the water of the seas; and let birds multiply on the earth.'...

Then God said, `Let the earth bring forth all kinds of living creatures: cattle, creeping things and wild animals of all kinds.' And so it happened. God made all kinds of animals, all kinds of cattle, and all kinds of creeping things of the earth. God saw how good it was... Then God said, `Let us make man in our image, after our likeness. Let them have dominion over the fish of the sea, the birds of the air, and the cattle, and over all the wild animals and all creature that crawl on the ground.

She closed the book. "The word of the Lord."

"Thanks be to God," the people said, reading from the program.

The professor from the university in cap and gown and wearing a white velvet hood, advanced to the podium. "Let us read Psalm 8 in unison," he said. We read,

> O Lord, our God, how glorious is your name over all the earth!
>
> You have exalted your majesty above the heavens.
>
> When I behold the heavens, the work of your fingers, the moon and the stars which you have set in place — what is man that you should be mindful of him or the son of man that you should care for him?
>
> You have given him rule over the works of his hands, putting all things under his feet: all sheep and oxen, yes, and beasts of the field, the birds of the air, the fishes of the sea and whatever swims in the paths of the sea.

When the professor turned his back to go to his seat, the people saw that his hood was lined in pink and blue, the colors of the university.

The president of the Humane Society, a slim brown-haired woman in a peach-colored dress, walked to the podium and announced she would read several intercessions to which the audience was to respond, "Blessed be God forever."

"God created us and placed us on this earth," she read, "to be the stewards of all living things and so to proclaim the glory of their Creator."

"Blessed be God forever."

"Blessed are you, O Lord, who for the sake of our comfort give us domestic animals as companions."

"Blessed be God forever," the congregation answered.

"Blessed are you, O Lord, who through your lowliest creatures never cease to draw us toward your love."

"Blessed be God forever."

The pastor of the First Lutheran Church, robed in white with a purple surplice, standing at the podium, said, "Let us pray.

"O God, you have done all things wisely; in your goodness you have made us in your image and given us care over other living things.

"Reach out your right hand and grant that these animals may serve our needs and that your bounty in the resources of this life may move us to seek more confidently the goal of eternal life.

"We ask this through Christ our Lord."

Everybody said, "Amen."

The clergymen on the platform came down among us and went to every animal.

Edith had been sleeping through the whole rite, but I woke her when one of the dignitaries approached, and he made a little cross with his finger on the top of her head and said, "Edith, I bless you in the name of the Lord." She looked up at him as if she understood what he was doing.

When all the animals had been blessed, the president of the seminary said the concluding prayer:

"May God, who created the animals of this earth as a help to us, continue to protect and sustain us with the grace his blessing brings, now and for ever, Amen."

The organist at the keyboard began playing the final hymn, which the people all sang:

> All things bright and beautiful,
> All creatures, great and small,
> All things wise and wonderful,
> the Lord God made them all.
>
> Each little flower that opens,
> each little bird that sings,
> he made their glowing colors,
> he made their tiny wings.
>
> The purple headed mountain,
> the river running by,
> the sunset, and the morning
> that brightens up the sky.

The cold wind in the winter,
the pleasant summer sun,
the ripe fruits in the garden,
He made them every one.

He gave us eyes to see them,
and lips that we might tell
How great is God Almighty,
Who has made all things well.

All things bright and beautiful,
all creatures great and small,
all things wise and wonderful,
the Lord God made them all.

"Go in peace," said the seminary president.
"Thanks be to God," we responded.
That was the end of the service.

Edith was ready to go home. I thought we ought to stay around for a while and talk to some of the other people, but she didn't agree. "Very well," she seemed to say, "if you won't take me, I'll walk." Dragging her leash behind her, she set off across the grass in the general direction of our home, twenty miles away.

I ran after her, grabbed her up and put her into her carrying case without a yowl of protest from her. There were no complaints as we drove back across town.

Edith has not changed since she was blessed. She remains a cat with flawless character except for a little furniture scratching.

As for me, I felt my character had improved after attending the rite.

It may be that is what the Blessing of the Animals is meant for.

Edith, wake up! It's time to get blessed.

ZZZZ

11.

Edith and Mrs. Gaskell's Cat

All over the world people with cats in their homes have common experiences. Cats tell you when they want to eat, which is all the time, or when they want to go out, which is three minutes after they came in. Now and then they lie down in front of you on their backs with their paws in prayerful attitudes and look fetching.

When they decide to sit on your lap, they turn all the way around before thumping into a catly lump. When they look into your eyes, they never blink.

People who live with cats are bonded together by that incomparable animal.

People who live with cats today have a bond, too, with other people who have lived with cats long before us. We can read about their adventures in the hundreds of books they have left behind them in the stores or the libraries.

One of those was Elizabeth Gaskell (1810-1865), English novelist and biographer, born in Chelsea, London. Her father was William Stevenson, a Unitarian minister, a farmer, editor of the *Scots Review*, and keeper of the records to the Treasury. His first wife, Elizabeth Holland, died when their baby Elizabeth was one month old. He took the infant to his wife's sister in the village of Knutsford, Cheshire, to be cared for. The little girl spent her childhood years in the village.

When she was seventeen, she returned to London to live with her father and his second wife. At twenty-five she married William Gaskell, a Unitarian minister and professor of English history and literature in Manchester New College. Elizabeth wanted to be a writer, and he encouraged her.

When their infant son died, she became depressed. William suggested that as therapy she should begin work on a book of fiction. The result was *Mary Barton, a History of Manchester*. It was published in two volumes in 1848 and gathered flattering reviews by Charles Dickens, Thomas Carlyle, and Walter Savage Landor.

Two years later Charles Dickens invited her to contribute to his new magazine, *Household Words*, and for the next three years in his magazine she wrote a series of sketches about life in the village of Knutsford where she grew up. In the sketches she called the village Cranford, and the stories sparkled with satire, humor, humor, and emotion. Critics have placed it in the same class as Jane Austen's works. If you haven't read *Cranford*, put it on your list of things to do. She wrote many other novels and an impressive two-volume biography of her friend Charlotte Bronte. She died in 1865, and is buried in the Unitarian churchyard of Knutsford.

Elizabeth Gaskell was a cat lover. One of her sketches in *Cranford* tells of an adventure a Mrs. Forrester had with her cat.

Mrs. Forrester owned an expensive lace collar, which she wore on her best dress. She was wearing it the day Lady Glassmire, one of Cranford's most socially prominent residents, came to call. Lady Glassmire commented on the beautiful lace.

"I daren't even trust the washing of it to my maid," she said. "I always wash it myself. Of course your ladyship knows that such lace must never be starched or ironed. Some people wash lace in sugar and water, and some in coffee to give it the right color, but I myself have a very good recipe for washing it in milk, which stiffens it enough and gives it a good, creamy color."

One morning Mrs. Forrester, preparing to wash the collar, poured out a bowl of milk and dropped the collar into it. Someone in an another part of the house called her, and she left the room.

When she came back, she found her cat crouched on the table, gulping as if she were choking.

"Oh, Pussy!" exclaimed Mrs. Forrester. "Poor Pussy, whatever is the matter with you?"

Then she saw the bowl of milk was empty.

"Oh, you naughty cat!" she shouted and slapped the cat, just as one slaps a choking child on the back. "It only helped the lace go down," Mrs. Forrester told Lady Glassmire.

"Whatever did you do?" inquired the lady.

"Strong measures were called for. I fetched a high top boot from my husband's wardrobe. I put the cat into it with her forefeet down so she could not scratch me. Then I mixed a teaspoon of emetic and a teaspoon of current jelly and insinuated it into her.

"I took her into the bedroom, put her on a clean towel, and sat down to wait. It was an anxious half-hour, Lady Glassmire. I could have kissed Pussy later when she presented me with the collar, very much as it was when it went down."

Mrs. Forrester gave the collar to her maid to boil it. Then she laid it on a lavender bush to dry. "And now, your ladyship," Mrs. Forrester said on concluding her story, "you would never know it has been in Pussy's insides."

A century later I had a similar experience and felt a kinship with Mrs. Forrester.

At a cat show I bought Edith a toy. It was a denim bow about two inches wide by one inch, fastened to a small fishing pole by a cord.

Edith chased the bow as I dangled it in front of her, catching it as it swung past her, biting the bow, letting it go and chasing it around the room and up over the chairs and sofa.

One day I rubbed a little fresh catnip on the bow.

She grabbed it in her mouth and pulled. I pulled.

Many times before she had caught the bow, clamped it on the floor with her paw and bit it. When she relaxed her grip, the bow flew out of her grasp, and she caught it again as it whizzed past her.

This time all at once I was holding a fishing pole with an empty piece of string dangling from it.

"Edith! I shouted.

Edith looked surprised.

The bow had vanished.

I dropped the rod and grabbed the cat. I pried her mouth open, hoping to get hold of the frayed bow before it went down.

There was nothing inside her mouth except her sharp teeth and her red tongue.

I called Dr. Coatney. "Bring her in," he said.

I broke the speed record driving down to his office.

He put her on his table and felt her all over. "I do not find a lump where the bow might be," he said. "Are you sure she swallowed it?"

"I'm sure. I saw it disappear down her throat."

"Was the bow fastened with a wire?"

"I don't know."

"If there is a piece of wire in it, it is a different matter."

One tasty bow.

He gave me a mixture of antibiotic and something to coat the lining of her stomach. "Watch her carefully until the bow appears," he said. "Likely you may never see it again. She may digest it."

I was not so fortunate as Mrs. Forrester. It took only a half hour for her to get her lace back.

I watched Edith for a whole week, but I never saw that bow again.

I had to cut a strip off the leg of a perfectly good pair of jeans to make Edith a new bow.

12.

Edith, the Thinker

Cat owners often look at their cats staring out of windows or lying with half open eyes on chairs or beds and wonder what their cats are thinking about or whether they think at all.

You may depend on it — cats do think.

A clump of fur developed on Edith's hip. Whenever I tried to comb it out, she winced and gave a hurt meow. In fact, she discouraged the combing by nipping my hand. She had a warm nose and did not want to play.

We went to see Dr. Coatney. He ran practiced fingers over the clump. "She has a sore spot there," he explained. The clump comes from licking the spot. She probably has an infection. We'll soon see."

He took his thermometer out of its sheath, and Edith eyed him. "I know," he said softly. "You don't like this. It won't take long."

Edith tolerated the thermometer with only a small complaint. When he read the figures, he whistled softly. "Yes, she has a fever. That means she has an infection. We'll have to give her a shot."

"How did she get an infection?"

"Something punctured her skin. Has she been walking close to any evergreens?"

On nice days I used to take Edith for walks in a cemetery close by. It is a pleasant garden-like spot protected from roads on two sides by a wrought iron fence that has roses and clematis growing on it. It is a peaceful place with little traffic on the driveways and carpeted with green grass and little beds of beautiful flowers. Edith walked close to the monuments and shrubbery. She liked to smell the taxus. "It could be a taxus needle or a thorn from a rose bush," said Dr. Coatney. "It got caught in her skin and became infected."

He gave me a bottle of penicillin. "Give her 500 milligrams twice a day," he instructed.

The way to give a cat liquid medicine, so they books say, is to get down on the floor and hold the cat between your knees so it can't back away. Tip up the cat's head with one hand and squeeze the medicine dropper into the corner of the cat's mouth with the other. I am not as agile as I was in days of yore, so I try to make giving medicine easier by having Edith jump up on a low chest where I can sit and clamp her between the wall and me.

It worked fine the first dose.

When Edith saw the medicine bottle the next time, she set her jaw and would have none of it. She wouldn't even jump up on the chest. All the sweet cajolery in my vocabulary could not persuade her to come near the chest.

I tried bribery.

Edith loved to eat grass when we used to walk in the cemetery. I also used to keep a pot of wheat sprouts for her growing on the window sill. Every morning I clipped a few sprouts and held them horizontally across her mouth so she could get a good grip on the grass. She chewed away with an expression of bliss on her face.

I sat down on the chest. Edith sat on the floor, looking up at me. I kept urging her to jump up and held out a few blades of the wheat sprouts.

She looked at the wheat sprouts. Longing showed in her green-gold eyes. Then she looked at the waiting medicine bottle. Back to the wheat sprouts her glance swiveled. Then she looked at the medicine.

wheat vs. medicine...

She sat there pondering.

73

I could almost see the thought chasing through her head. "The wheat tastes good, but the medicine tastes horrible. Do I want the wheat badly enough to take the medicine?"

She sat there, pondering. Then she walked into the closet and curled up on the carpet.

After a while I pretended to give up. I went about the household chores, and then I went into the bedroom and clipped off a few strands of wheat and called her.

Her desire for the wheat overcame her fear of the medicine and she hopped up on the chest. After she had her wheat, I grabbed her, clamped her to the wall and jabbed the medicine dropper into the corner of her mouth. You may wonder why I didn't just grab Edith off the floor and make her take the medicine. If I tried to pick Edith up, I knew from experience what would happen. She would dive under the bed, and there is no way in this world for a woman to get Edith out from under the bed if she doesn't want to come.

We played out the little scenario twice a day for a week with Edith sitting on the floor watching me hold out the tempting, succulent grass to her.

One morning the tableau lasted twenty minutes. Finally I gave up because I had a dental appointment.

"Very well," I said, dropping the grass clippings

into the waste basket. "You ought to take your medicine. It will make you feel better. It is for your own good. I realize you don't understand that. But I can't stand here all day waiting for you to make up your mind. I have to leave in a few minutes to go to the dentist. We will try again tonight."

I turned to make the bed.

Edith walked out of the room, and I started to dress.

When I was putting on my makeup in the bathroom, I noticed Edith sitting at my feet, looking up into my face. "What do you want, Edith?"

Edith walked over to the chest and jumped up on it.

I gave her some wheat and then picked up the medicine bottle. I didn't even have to clamp her to the wall. I sat down beside her, holding the

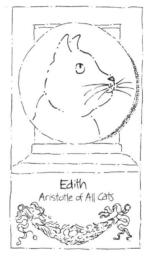

Edith
Aristotle of All Cats

medicine dropper to the corner of her mouth. She opened her lips and down her throat went the medicine.

"Good girl!" I hugged her and we went to the kitchen to get her a treat.

She had thought it over, and she decided that to get her wheat she would have to take the medicine.

Edith is the Aristotle of all cats.

13.

Einstein Edith

Very early in our association Edith gave another splendid example of her thinking ability. It happened only about two weeks after I brought her home from the adoption center.

I had planned to go on a two-week trip to Ireland. As the day of departure approached, I wished I were not going.

The reason was Edith.

I had arranged for my friends Catharine and Lewis to take Edith into their home while I was gone. She knew them, and she liked their cat Blackwell. They could play together and explore the woods behind the house.

When I brought out my suitcases and laid them opened on the dining room table, Edith came running. Oh, joy! Something new had appeared. She jumped up on the table, sniffed at every inch of the bags and tried them out as napping places. She inspected everything that went into them: blouses, sweaters, skirts. She seemed so joyful that my spirits began to wilt. She didn't know that she was not going with me.

The night before I was to leave, I packed a bag with Edith's belongings: food for two weeks, her comb and brush, an extra collar, several toys and her special water bowl with her name on it.

When I opened Edith's carrying case, she didn't want to go into it. I pointed her in the right direction and gave a little push. I felt like a traitor.

It was two miles through a twisting, wooded road from our house to Catharine's. Edith stared out of her carrying case at me and cried all the way.

Once at Catharine's house, Edith checked out Blackwell's food bowl, helped herself to a little and settled down to take a nap in the best wing chair.

"We won't tell you if anything goes wrong," said Catharine as I got into the car to leave. "It would spoil your trip."

It was an empty house I went back to. Nobody landed on the bed in the middle of the night. No little voice said, "Meow" when the alarm went off in the morning. If I hadn't already paid for my ticket and told the Irish I was coming, I would have stayed home.

The horrible thing is something did go wrong. For three days after I left, Catharine said, Edith moped around, refusing to eat or to go outdoors to play with Blackwell. On the fourth day, however, she perked up, ate Blackwell's food and her own, too, and followed Blackwell outside to play on the wooded hillside.

At the end of the first week, Catharine had to go out of town for a few days. The plan was for Lewis to leave the cats outside while he went to his office for the day. He would leave food and water in the open garage. When he came home at dinnertime, he and the cats would spend the evening and night together in the house.

Catharine left on Wednesday evening. The next morning Lewis put the cats out and went to the office. When he returned in the early evening, only one cat was waiting for him. "Where is Edith?" Lewis asked Blackwell.

He called her a few times, but she did not come. "She will come back before bedtime," Lewis told Blackwell.

She did not come back all evening. He waited up for her until midnight. "She will be here in the morning," Lewis told Blackwell and turned out the lights.

The minute he woke on Friday morning, he went downstairs to look for Edith.

She was not waiting on the windowsill or on the front stoop.

Lewis called the police department and reported that Edith, a brown-and-orange tabby wearing a collar with his telephone number on it, had wandered away.

The officer said if the police found her, he would notify Lewis.

In the middle of the morning his nurse reported — Lewis was a physician — that the police had found a declawed tabby.

"No, that's not Edith," he said. "She has her claws."

He drove all around the neighborhood that night, calling Edith.

She had not returned on Saturday morning. He was not on call that Saturday so he spent the day walking through the neighborhood looking under bushes and calling Edith's name.

"Could she have gone back home?" a neighbor asked.

"She wouldn't know the way," said Lewis. "She lives two miles from here, and she has never even seen out of the car windows when Roz drove her up here because she keeps her in her carrying case. But I'll check it out."

He drove to our house and checked the property, calling Edith plaintively. Nobody answered.

He drove back home disconsolate. Edith hadn't had anything to eat since she left. Had she been hit by a car? Was she lying injured somewhere or worse, dead?

Sunday morning when Lewis opened the door to let Blackwell out, there on the step sat Edith. She rushed into the house, dashed to the food bar, ate a good meal, hopped into the wing chair and went to sleep.

She slept all day Sunday.

Next morning she went out on the hill with Blackwell, and when Lewis came home that night, she was there. Catharine came home on Tuesday morning and from then on the two cats played on the hillside, came in when they were hungry, biffed each other a few times, chased each other through the house in the early evening and settled down to a comfortable life.

When I arrived home at the end of two weeks, I didn't even stop to unpack my suitcases. I jumped into my car and drove up through the twisted road through the woods to Catharine's house.

When I drove into the driveway, Edith came running around the house.

"Meow," she said, and jumped into the car as soon as I opened the door. I picked her up and hugged her.

When a little later after I heard what happened, I opened the door to her carrying case, she didn't have to be pushed to go inside. She was going home!

I wrote a column about how Edith had disappeared while I was gone.

When it appeared, my next door neighbor Willa rang the doorbell. She had the paper in her hand. "I am so appalled I hardly know what to say," she began.

"What's wrong?" I asked. "Come in and tell me."

"I was working in my garden last Friday morning," she said when we sat down with coffee on the back patio. "I had dissolved some fertilizer in a bucket of water and was giving my flowers a drink. The phone rang, and I hurried into the house to answer it. When I came back out, there was Edith, drinking out of the bucket.

"'You mustn't drink that, Edith,' I told her. `I'll get you some fresh water.'

"I put the fertilizer water out of her reach, and she drank and drank and drank the fresh water."

Wile Edith was drinking, Willa read the label on the fertilizer bottle. To her horror, the label warned: "Poisonous to people and animals."

Willa dashed into the house and called the poison control office. "The woman who answered was very nice," Willa said. "She didn't mind at all that I called about a cat and not a child. She looked up the poison and said she thought Edith would be all right as long as she had drunk so much clean water right after she drank the fertilizer water. She might have a sore mouth or tongue for a while."

Edith stayed around for a long time while Willa worked with her plants.

When Willa finished and went into the house, Edith tried to come in with her.

"I didn't let her come in," she said, "because she might find some rubber bands on the floor. I told her to go home. I didn't know you were away. When I think how Edith came to me for help and I turned her away, I could cry. Don't you ever dare go away again without letting me know."

I do not know how Edith ever found her way down the two miles from Catharine's house to our house or how long it took her to walk those two miles. What is even more remarkable is that when she found I was not at home and Willa wouldn't help her, she walked two more miles all the way back to Catharine's house.

If that isn't an example of a thinking mind, I'll eat my hat.

14.

The Hearing Aid Mystery

One of the most flawed bits of poetic thinking Robert Browning is responsible for, in my opinion, is

> Grow old along with me!
> The best is yet to be,
> The last of life, for which the first was made

He wrote that in 1864 when he was fifty-two years of age, and you'd think he would have known better by that time.

If you keep on breathing, you will get old. When you get old, all manner of embarrassing things happen to your body. One of them is your senses start to go. You have to get spectacles to read. Then you have to get hearing aids to make sense of what people are telling you at cocktail parties and what stiff-jawed television commentators are saying.

I finally had to get hearing aids for each ear. They are extremely complicated bits of machinery and dreadfully expensive.

They are also just the right size for cats to play with. My tabby cat Edith likes to bat them off the night stand and roll them around on the carpet almost as well as she likes to play with rubber bands.

One Sunday morning I had been reading the newspaper in bed when I heard Edith playing with a hearing aid. Half an hour later when I finished the paper and rose to resume life, the hearing aid had disappeared from the night stand. I gave the carpet a cursory glance, but it is the same color as the hearing aid.

Edith and I went out to the kitchen for breakfast, and she ate heartily as usual.

After breakfast we followed our usual routine, which is for me to brush her coat backwards and forwards while she stands on the chest by the window. I give her the hairball prevention medicine, which she views as the treat of the day. Then I make the bed.

As soon as the bedspread was back in place that morning, I looked for the hearing aid.

It was not on the floor around the night stand. It was not under the dresser. It was not under the chest nor the chiffonier. It was not in the closet, under the bed, or behind the clothes hamper. It was not in the bathroom off the bedroom.

Then Edith threw up her breakfast all over the pale beige carpet.

"Edith! Why did you throw up? Did you swallow my hearing aid?"

She said nothing.

I hurried into the living room to get the book on cat care. Panic was beginning to set in, not so much about the two-thousand-dollar hearing aid but about the priceless cat.

The book lists things a cat will swallow: small stones, marbles, parts of toys, nuts, olive pits, pieces of plastic wrap, bits of aluminum foil, needles, pins, fish hooks, thread, yarn, and strings from roasts.

It didn't say anything about hearing aids.

A hearing aid is about the size of a marble. The battery case was open when I put the hearing aid on the night stand, and if Edith had swallowed it, I reasoned the battery could come loose in her interior and cause more trouble than the hearing aid itself.

Edith was not choking or showing any kind of distress except she had thrown up.

The book said that some times a swallowed object causes no problem, but if over a twenty-four hour period there are any signs of distress or any vomiting, the cat should be taken to the vet. "By all means you shouldn't act with hysteria or haste," said the book, "but be sure to act."

What good does it do for a book to tell you not to act with hysteria? When it is your cat who may have swallowed a hearing aid and have a toxic battery disintegrating in her insides, it is hard not to be attacked by hysteria.

You do not, however, call a veterinarian on Sunday if you can avoid it. I gave Edith a little bit of food and decided to go on to church, but if she threw up again, I would call Dr. Coatney, Sunday or not.

I told everybody at church about what happened and prayed for Edith when we said the prayers for the people. Catharine came home with me from church and searched the whole apartment on her hands and knees with the flashlight. The hearing aid was not in the apartment, but Edith had not thrown up her second breakfast.

Nothing like a little $800 toy!

Beep Beep

"I think you'd better call Dr. Coatney just to be on the safe side," Catharine advised.

He was at home, enjoying a day off. "Are you sure she swallowed it?" he asked. "I say that because I get lots of calls about hearing aids, but so far they have all turned up."

"I am sure," I answered. I told him how she had thrown up her breakfast right after she swallowed the hearing aid.

"Give her little amounts of food and water," he said. "If she throws up again, call me, but if she does not, bring her to the office in the morning and we will take an x-ray and go from there."

I felt better right away.

Next morning I spent an hour crawling on the floor, feeling behind dresser legs, putting my eye as near to the floor surface as I could and sweeping the carpet with a flashlight. That hearing aid was not in the apartment.

Edith and I were waiting when Dr. Coatney's office opened. He took her to the x-ray room and I sat looking over the other patients as they came in. One man had a big, flat, square box.

"Is there anything in your box?" I asked him.

He opened the box. Inside with a blanket wrapped around him was a land turtle about sixteen inches across.

"My goodness. What is wrong with him?"

"He has a cold," said his owner.

I thought about that for a time. "How can you tell when a turtle has a cold?"

"He sneezes, and his nose runs."

After a long time Dr. Coatney opened his door and summoned me inside his examining room. "Edith did not swallow your hearing aid," he said. He showed me the x-ray and pointed out her stomach, her digestive tract and her intestines.

I was chagrined. "Anyhow, we have a complete x-ray for her files," he pointed out cheerfully.

I had invited Freda to dinner that night. When she arrived, I told her about the hearing aid mystery.

"I will find the hearing aid," she said.

She went into the bedroom and stood looking around. She picked up the clothes hamper and moved it bodily away from the wall. "Here it is," she said.

"How did you ever think to pick up the clothes hamper?" I asked, marveling.

"Something just told me. I have found scores of little things my cat Sarah has batted under my clothes hamper."

Later I mentioned the adventure to the woman who sold me my hearing aids.

"You should have called me. How much did the x-ray cost?"

"Fifty dollars."

"I could have saved you that and all your worry."

"How so?"

"I have been in this business for thirty-five years," she said, "and I know. Cats love to play with hearing aids because they hear a faint buzzing coming from the aid that a person can't hear. Now dogs are different. Dogs swallow hearing aids all the time, and we always warn our patients who have dogs they must be extremely careful. But cats — cats never swallow hearing aids."

15.

Edith and the New Upholstery

The living room had begun to look like its owner, a bit old and tacky.

The springs in the furniture had sagged somewhat with years of sitting, and here I admit an amount of similarity. Life is one process of losing the battle with the force of gravity and many things about me sag.

I called an upholsterer to come look at the furniture. "If you have the furniture reupholstered," he said, "it will look better and be better than if you bought new, although it will cost more to have it redone."

"How much?"

The figures staggered me a little, but since two of the chairs were irreplaceable chairs from my grandmother and the lines of the other chairs and the sofa were beautiful, and as I wouldn't have to go around to stores shopping, I said, "How long will the furniture be gone?"

"Several weeks."

"Gee. That's a long time to be without furniture."

"I will bring you a chair to sit on."

"All right, then."

He sent the men to haul away the sofa, two upholstered chairs and two dining room chairs and brought one upholstered chair from his shop for me to use.

Edith watched the workmen carry the four chairs and the sofa away. She walked forlornly around the nearly empty room and then hopped up into the upholsterer's chair and took a nap. That left one place for me to sit — the floor. For several days I watched television in the evening on the floor with my back propped against the wall.

One evening a friend in the apartment building knocked and opened the door. She stood looking at the tableau.

"There is something wrong with this picture," she remarked. "Why doesn't Edith sit on the floor and Roz sit in the chair?"

It is hard to explain to anybody who does not have a cat. Say what you will about society, altruism, modesty, and unselfishness, when it comes down to the last word, we all think of ourselves as the main player on our own stage.

Cats are no different from people in this. Edith thinks she is the important person in our house. She has no way of understanding that it is not polite for her to take the only living room chair in the living room. If I am writing checks at my desk, it would be considerate of her not to sit down on the check book or to scratch her chin on the end of the pen, even while I am writing with it, but she does not understand that.

Smart as she is, Edith has never learned to read. She does not care for television. She has few ways to pass the time except to stare out the door, play a little with her toys, and take naps. That is why I let her sit in the only chair. If she finds pleasure in sitting on my check book, I wait and write checks when she is doing something else.

After about a month the upholsterer brought the furniture back. It was beautiful. The sofa and one chair were upholstered in white with brown wood trimming. Edith is brown and knows, I think, that she looks perfectly splendid against the sofa's white upholstery. The wing chair, the one I bought expressly for her, is covered in a pale blue fabric with muted pale pink and green brush marks like an impressionist painting. She does not sit or lie in it; Edith takes the white furniture and Roz sits in the blue chair. I can't even see the television set from it.

When we were still living in the house on Springhill, I replaced the shag carpeting that came with the house with newer, prettier carpet. When the new, pale carpet was in place, all the furniture in the room looked shabby. I gave the old sofa and its companion chair and the old wing chair to the Salvation Army. I replaced the sofa and its matching chair. Edith took offense when I gave away the wing chair she always slept in and started sulking in the kitchen, sleeping on the hard, brick floor. She did not return to the living room for two months.

One day I was walking through a furniture department in a downtown store when I saw a lovely wing chair, just the right size and color for Edith. It was a kind of magenta color, and wouldn't show the dirt, and I thought she would love it, stop sulking, and return to the living room.

A saleswoman, who told me her name was Gloria, came past and began talking about the good points of the chair. "Sit in it," she suggested, "and see how comfortable it is."

I tried it, and it was comfortable. "The chair is not for me," I told her. "It is for Edith."

"Then it would be wise for Edith to come in and sit in it before you buy it," said Gloria. "We always ask the person who will sit in the chair to try it out. That way we avoid delivering a chair that is unsuitable and having to pick it up again."

"Edith is my cat," I said.

Gloria stared at me somewhat askance. "I suggest in that case," she said, "that you have the chair Scotch-guarded."

I did as she suggested and when the store delivered the chair, I had the delivery men put it in the same place the old chair occupied.

Edith came in after the delivery men left and sniffed at the new chair. She has never sat or napped in it from that day until this one. I asked her why not, but Edith stands on her constitutional rights to remain silent. This is the same wing chair, now expensively reupholstered, that Edith continues to ignore.

Sometimes when we don't have company and I have caught up with my work and reading, I like to watch a television program. I usually sit on the sofa to do it, and after a while I think, "It would be more comfortable to watch this lying down." So I put a towel on the pale blue cushion that matches Edith's chair, and I slip off my shoes because I don't want any dirt to get on the white sofa. I watch only edifying programs, and pretty soon I am edified right into somnolence. Edith spends the evening in the top of her floor-to-ceiling tree if somebody is using the white furniture.

At exactly nine o'clock she comes down from the tree for her evening snack. She sits in front of the sofa for a moment or two, staring at the snoozing giant.

"Scratch, scratch, scratch" she goes, right on the brand new, highly expensive sofa.

I leap awake, shout that she mustn't do that, and get up to get her snack.

The only way I can keep her from scratching the upholstery is to sit upright and keep awake. Even so, sitting straight upright with my feet on the floor, I sometimes doze off, with my head drooping on my neck like some overripe sunflower.

"Scratch, scratch, scratch."

I leap awake, but the highly expensive white upholstery is beginning to fray again.

I am casting about for ways to solve the problem. I have considered setting an alarm clock to wake me about five minutes before Miss Scratcher starts to descend her tree.

Or I could go back to sitting on the floor again.

16.

Edith and the Bean Juice

Edith is an eternal optimist. She has been on a diet for eight years ever since she became an apartment cat. She still thinks, however, that if she looks wistful enough and sits by her empty food bowl long enough, somebody will relent and put a little extra food in it.

Once in a long while she jumps up on the counter at breakfast time and puts her nose right down on the can of meat as I open it, filling her lungs with the tantalizing fragrance of beef or chicken or fish. Otherwise, she has forsaken her kittenish ways of walking on the counter.

I thought she had, that is.

Once when she was very young, I made broccoli soufflé for guests. I cooked the broccoli until it was just done but still crisp and added it to a white sauce into which I stirred the yolks of six eggs. I beat the egg whites to a stiff froth and folded them into the soufflé. I lit the oven and had just finished piling the concoction into a soufflé dish when the front doorbell rang.

In trooped the guests and for a few minutes I was busy hanging up coats in the guest closet and taking drink orders around the living room.

When I returned to the kitchen to make the drinks and put the soufflé into the oven, there sat Edith on the counter, washing her face. All around the edge of the soufflé were scalloped indentations that had been made by Edith's little red tongue.

I stood there appalled. I did not scold Edith, for the guests would have heard me, and she wouldn't have known what I was scolding her for anyhow. It was entirely too late to make another soufflé. I smoothed out the soufflé with a spatula and put it into the oven. We were four at the table that evening; nobody ever knew that the soufflé had served five.

No doubt some people will be horrified at this.

Yet I recall reading the confession in an Ann Landers column once of a woman who found herself with drinks for her bridge club but no hors d'oeuvres.

She opened a box of crackers, spread them with chicken pate from her cat's store of canned food, and toasted them slightly. One of the guests loved the hors d'oeuvres so much that she was begging for the recipe. The woman asked Ann whether she should tell her the truth. Ann advised her against it.

One of my friends told me he had hired an office girl once who brought her lunch to work and always opened a can of cat food to eat with her bread-and-butter sandwich.

I have never tasted any of Edith's food, but some of it smells extremely good.

On to the bean juice story. Twelve years have passed since the soufflé incident, and never once since then has Edith sampled any of the food on the counter until —

I made a beaner-wiener sandwich for Catharine.

To make the sandwich slice a loaf of French bread lengthwise, spread with mustard butter and cover with Boston baked beans with a little chopped onion and brown sugar added. On top make a layer of sliced wieners and grated cheese. Broil until the cheese is melted. Serve with bread-and-butter pickles.

I placed everything on the counter ready to assemble when Catharine arrived. We watched a garden show on television for half an hour. When I went to the kitchen, there sat Edith, crouched over the bean bowl, her little tongue going in and out like anything, lapping up the bean juice.

What to do? I had no more beans.

I remembered the soufflé. I spread the beans on the French bread, assembled the rest of the sandwich and broiled it.

It was a very good sandwich.

Later I confessed to Catharine what had happened.

"I don't mind at all," she said. "I have a cat at home."

Actually, Edith had helped. The beans were supposed to be drained before putting them in the sandwich.

Edith saved me from having to wash and dry the drainer.

17.

Elevator Adventure

Our apartment is on what is called the Lake Level, which means it is down a flight of steps from the first floor where everybody enters. In other words we live in the basement, but the staff turns pale if anybody calls it that. After all, to live on the Lake Level with a walk-out patio where the geese and the ducks play, costs more than to live up above, so it must never, never be called the basement.

Right opposite our hall door is the elevator. Once a month I put Edith in her carrying case and take her up on the elevator to the first floor and out to the garage. We go for her monthly checkup with Dr. Coatney.

One gorgeous April day when the daffodils were blooming and the flowering crabs made the very air around the lake pink and white with their blossoms, and the blue sky overhead with the floating white puffy clouds was reflected in the lake, we came back from Dr. Coatney's office in a happy mood. The next item on the day's agenda was lunch, which is one of Edith's favorite activities. We were happy. All was right with our world.

I punched the elevator button. It seemed an inordinately long time before the elevator door slid open and we stepped inside. The door closed. I punched the button marked LL.

When it was time for us to be there, the door did not open.

I stood there waiting. Still the door did not open.

I set Edith's case down on the floor.

I looked at the panel of buttons on the inside of the elevator door. The little square that said 1 was lighted. We were still on the first floor.

"That's funny," I said to Edith. "I must have forgot to punch the button."

I punched LL.

When it was time for us to arrive on the lake level, the door did not open.

"Well," said I, picking up the case, "I think we'd better get out of this elevator. I punched 1.

Nothing happened. It began to dawn on me that we were stuck, as idle as Coleridge's painted ship upon the painted ocean.

"Maybe we can go up," I said to Edith and punched 2.

I put her case down again.

I jumped up and down, trying to jiggle the elevator into action.

Nothing happened.

I remembered that once one of the other residents was stuck for half a day in the elevator and afterwards the maintenance department issued a paper on what to do when stuck in the elevator, but I had forgot what it said.

"The thing to do, Edith," I said, "is to keep calm."

Edith was getting tired and began yowling.

I looked at the plate of buttons on front of me. One said "Cancel call." I punched it.

Nothing happened.

Then I noticed one with a picture of a bell on it. I punched it.

A bell rang out, loud and clear.

"Cheer up, Edith," I told her. "Help is on the way."

Nothing happened.

I rang the bell again, only I gave three punches instead of one. "What's the Morse Code for Help?" I asked Edith. "I think it is S. O. S., but I don't remember how to punch the letters."

Nothing happened.

I was getting tired. "They ought to have seats in elevators," I said to Edith. "They have seats in the elevators in the Savoy in London," I told her. I don't know why I thought she might be interested in that piece of information, but I thought the sound of my voice might reassure her. There really are seats in the elevators in the Savoy. I went there once for lunch. You don't forget that kind of thing.

"Surely somebody will find us some time," I said to Edith. "I just hope it is before dinner time."

Edith continued to yowl.

Then I noticed a little picture of a telephone on the panel.

There was, however, no telephone. But there was a kind of blank space, and I felt with a finger along the edge of it and found a little door that opened. Behind the panel was a telephone.

I picked it up and held it to my ear.

A dial tone sounded. "Cheer up, Edith, help is at hand."

Then I stood looking at the telephone. On the first floor at the main entrance is a desk at which a receptionist sits. I did not, however, know the number of the telephone that sit on the desk in front of her. There was no telephone book in the elevator.

Then I remembered that it was Wednesday, the day when Dorothy cleans our apartment. I dialed the number to my apartment.

The telephone rang.

And rang.

And rang.

My answering machine came on. It told me that Roz was not at home, but she will return your call if you leave your name and number.

I dialed my number again.

"Hello?" said a voice.

"This is Roz," I said. "I am stuck in the elevator."

"What?"

"I am stuck in the elevator."

"How did you do that?"

"I don't know. Something must be wrong with it. Get help."

"Where is Edith?"

"She is here in the elevator with me."

"Oh. What should I do?"

"You could call Janis on the desk upstairs and tell her."

"Janis. Is that the woman in the lobby?"

"Yes."

"What's her number?"

"I don't know. Go up to the lobby and tell her I am stuck in the elevator."

She hung up.

Nothing happened.

I was getting tired standing in the elevator. I could sit down on the floor, but there is no way I could get to my feet gracefully from sitting on the elevator floor.

I might not even be able to get to my feet at all. Besides, when the elevator door did finally slide open, I was pretty certain there would be a crowd of spectators gathered outside.

"This is ridiculous," I told Edith. I dialed our number again.

"Hello?"

"Did you get help?"

"No. I pushed the button, but the elevator is not working."

"I know that," I said, trying to keep from shouting. "Now listen. Walk down the hall and then walk up the steps to the lobby. Tell the woman who is sitting there that Roz is stuck in the elevator."

"Oh," she said.

The line went dead.

We waited. I read all the notices about birthdays and concerts on the bulletin board in the elevator. I wished I had brought a book with me, but I doubt there is any book I know of that could hold my attention while waiting to be rescued from the elevator.

I stood and stood and stood, and Edith yowled and yowled and yowled.

The petty pace of minutes crept by to the last syllable of recorded time.

At that moment the lights in the elevator went off. I could feel the irises in my eyes expanding.

Then the elevator door opened.

Five men from the maintenance department stood facing me and grinning.

I do not understand the human race. For some reason people who are not stuck in an elevator think that people who get stuck in one are funny or doing it for laughs.

It is not funny. It took me the rest of the day to regain my usually sunny disposition.

Edith did not think it was funny, either, although she didn't say anything. She ate her lunch and then took a nap on the sofa.

18.

Edith and the Chipmunk

Last spring a chipmunk built a nest under the patio of my next-door neighbor. The chipmunks used my patio as a short cut to wherever they went shopping or for strolls in the garden.

One afternoon Edith on her leash was lying in the mulch by a pot of parsley.

In her youth Edith had a number of chipmunk adventures. She caught a baby one once and brought it into the house and dropped it into the bathtub. Another time she caught one and ate the whole thing right under our picture window. Since she moved to Bethany, however, she had not even so much as seen one for eight years. You would think she had forgotten about them.

The neighbor's chipmunk had been out on some errand or other and cut across our garden to return home by way of our patio.

111

The chipmunk probably didn't even see Edith because she is the same color as the mulch. I was reading a book under the patio umbrella.

The telephone rang. I went inside, leaving the door open a bit because Edith always follows me wherever I go, even to the bathroom. She followed me in and dropped a chipmunk on the carpet.

That chipmunk dashed across the floor past me and into the foyer with Edith loping after him. I let the answering machine take over the telephone while I ran after chipmunk and cat.

The chipmunk ran into the bedroom and disappeared. Edith paced back and forth along the chest where I groom her.

I supposed the chipmunk, his heart thumping with fright, crouched under the chest.

If I moved the chest, Edith would catch the chipmunk and I could pick her up with him in her mouth and take them both outside, where I could probably persuade Edith to let him go.

I moved the chest gingerly out from the wall, but no chipmunk appeared.

I am an old hand at searching under the furniture in our apartment, having had so much experience with a game Edith likes to play with hearing aids. I did not find the chipmunk.

Edith went back into the living room to take a nap on the white chair, and I sat down to consider what to do about the chipmunk. I did not want it to take up residence in the apartment. I could imagine how it would feel to be wakened during the night by a chipmunk chased by a cat both romping around in the bed.

There are sixty-eight apartments in our building. In every one lives somebody who would not like to be told there is a chipmunk in the building. I felt I'd better not telephone for help in getting the chipmunk out because then pretty soon everybody would know, and there might even be hysterics or a few nervous breakdowns. Some of the people even call up distraught if they see so much as a spider in the trash room.

Between the bottom of the hall door to my apartment and the hallway there is a space about one inch high. It was my hope that when I turned the lights out to go to bed and everything got quiet in our apartment, the chipmunk might venture out, and attracted by the strip of light under the door, he would escape into the rest of the building somewhere. I would not tell a soul what had happened, and if I heard talk about a chipmunk loose in the building, I would be as surprised as anyone how it managed to get in.

The first night passed with no sign of the chipmunk.

A day passed with no evidence appearing that

the chipmunk was in my apartment.

The second night passed without incident.

The next morning after breakfast Edith jumped up on the chest for her grooming.

There on the window sill lay three little black chips of something that had not been there before.

My heart sank.

The chipmunk had left those little black chips. He was still in the apartment!

Then a thought struck me. I could leave the window open and take off the screen, and the next time the chipmunk hopped up on the window sill, he could escape out the open window.

There was one thing wrong with that plan.

The chipmunk moved from my bedroom during the night and went out into the kitchen. I found some more little black chips the next morning on the counter.

I began to worry. A kitchen has many places for a chipmunk to hide. He could go under the dishwasher or the refrigerator or climb into a cupboard. I had to get him out of there.

I called the emergency number of the maintenance department and when someone answered, I said, "I need a small animal trap in my apartment."

The woman who took my call did not ask why. "I will relay your message," she said.

In about half an hour somebody knocked on

my door and handed me a trap. He did not ask what I wanted it for. I volunteered no information.

I set the trap on the floor and baited it with peanut butter spread on a cracker. I shut Edith up in the office.

Then I went out onto the patio and sat down to read a book.

Half an hour later I went into the apartment and into the kitchen.

The trap door was down.

Inside the trap sat a frightened chipmunk.

I picked up the trap and carried it outside.

My neighbors were on the patio having lunch. They looked at me curiously as I set the trap down in the grass and opened the door.

Out popped the chipmunk. He scurried across their patio and disappeared into his nest.

My neighbor did not ask how I happened to be bringing a chipmunk out of my apartment, and I did not explain.

I called for the trap to be picked up, and life resumed its placid way in our apartment. Until this day I have never told a soul about the adventure although I hated not to write a column about it. But ever in my mind I hear that "You and your damned cat have ruined Bethany," and it makes me cautious.

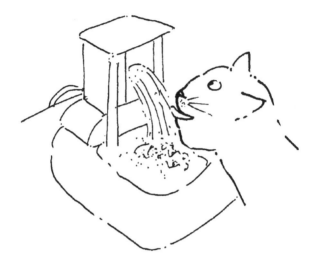

19.

The Drinker

Edith reminds me of the Duke in *As You Like It*, who found books in the running brooks. Right from the beginning she enjoyed the gushing garden hose, the dripping downspout, the cascading faucet and the swirling sink drain. She peers into running water with the intensity of a Louis Pasteur staring into a microscope.

One morning she leaped onto the sink and crouched on the chopping block to watch the water gush out of the faucet. She stuck her nose into the stream, and out came that little red tongue. She took one hundred and fifty-six sips, ran her tongue over her lips and sat back, looking at me as if to say, "that is what I like best."

"Edith," I said, "you have a special bowl with your name on it filled with nice, fresh drinking water. Why don't you drink out of it? Drinking out of the faucet wastes water. Water costs money, to say nothing of the sewer rent charges."

Next morning she hopped up on the chopping block again, ready for another drink. Instead of turning on the faucet, I filled a two-quart watering can for potted plants and poured. She took one hundred twelve sips before the can was empty. I refilled it and she took forty-five more.

When we lived on Springhill and had a bathtub, Edith perched on the rim while I had my bath. She leaned far out over the water and sniffed at the bath suds. Once she slipped and fell in and leaped out again, her fur coat all soapy and her tail like a fluff of cotton candy. When I finished bathing, she stayed behind to watch the water drain out of the tub.

I have found her drinking from the downspout during rains, and from a fountain we had in the back yard every time I turned on the pump that circulated the water.

Once when I had a new toilet installed in the old house, it kept flushing at odd times of the day and night when nobody was using it.

I called the plumber to come back to find out what was wrong. "If this keeps up," I told him, "the water bill will bankrupt me."

He came, and he tinkered around in the bathroom a long time. At last he came into the living room where I was and said, "I'm sorry, Mrs. Young, but I simply cannot find anything wrong with your toilet."

He started writing the bill for his service call when the toilet flushed.

We both bolted for the bathroom. There sat Edith, watching as the water swirled around in the bowl. She had figured out had to trip the handle on the new toilet. The plumber replaced it with an old-fashioned handle, and that was the end of the case of the toilet that flushed itself.

I have several bonsai plants that require drinks about once a day or more often in hot weather. Sometimes I forget to water them and find one or more of them keeled over in a faint.

I devised a way they can water themselves. I put a blue pottery bowl on the plant stand and buried two strands of shoelaces in the soil of each plant and dangled the rest of the laces in the blue pottery, which held enough water for several days. The plants watered themselves by capillary attraction.

I has amazed at how the water level in the blue pottery bowl went down. Those four plants drank at least four pints of water every other day.

One Saturday morning as I sat on the floor by the window reading the newspaper, I heard the sound of water lapping. I thought perhaps something was leaking, and headed for the sound of the water.

There sat Edith, drinking out of the plants' bowl.

After we moved to Bethany, Edith lost all of her sources for running water. There was no tub, and the spout on the kitchen sink faucet is too long for her to reach comfortably. We have no outdoors fountain now and no dripping downspouts. She has the porcelain drinking bowl with her name on it in the kitchen. She always came running whenever I watered the plants in the window and tried to get a drink from the watering can, but I don't want her drinking water in which I have dissolved fertilizer.

I had a lovely soup bowl of Limoges china with hand painted roses on it and a lot of gold leaf all around the edge. I set it on the plant stand and she learned to drink from it instead of the watering can.

One day among the advertisements in my cat magazine a question caught my glance. "Does Your Cat Want Running Water?" the caption across the top of the ad asked. Beneath the question was a photo of a cat drinking from a cascade of water running into a bowl. The filtered water in the bowl is constantly recirculated by a little electric pump.

The cat drinking fountain would fit in the place where I keep the Limoges bowl.

I sent in an order.

When the box arrived, Edith inspected the entire contents and watched me put the drinking

fountain together. I filled the bowl with water —
not out of the kitchen faucet but from the one in
the residents' dining room that provides better tast-
ing water than the faucets in our apartments do. I
set it on the plant stand and put it beside her Limoges
bowl. I turned on the recirculating pump and sat
back to watch Edith.

The little cascade makes a nice, trickling noise.
Edith looked at the fountain and walked over to her
old, placid pool of water in her regular bowl and
drank.

It took two days before she ventured to drink
from her new drinking fountain, but soon she was
drinking from it all the time. I have put the Limoges
bowl away in the cupboard.

The fountain even has a place to drop an ice
cube in to cool the water on a hot day, and has a
filter, too, to keep the water purified.

What more could any cat want?

Edith has gastritis.

20.

Pepto Pink

Edith developed a delicate digestive system. She threw up frequently.

I had to stop raising her little pots of wheat sprouts because although she ate the wheat with relish, she threw it up the next morning.

After we moved to Bethany and I took Edith for walks in the cemetery, she ate the grass there, too, and threw it up. So I stopped taking her for cemetery walks.

Edith is a clean cat who gives herself frequent baths. Whenever she wakes from a nap, she gives herself a washing all over. Sometimes when she gets embarrassed, as when she misses me and comes to hunt me up and we run into each other in the hallway, she doesn't want me to know she was looking for me, so she sits down and washes.

Twice a day she has a quarter can of meat to

eat and when she finishes, she runs her little pink tongue over her lips on an average of thirty-seven times. That make an average of seventy-four licks a day on her muzzle alone.

I lay a towel over my bedspread for Edith to sleep on, and for a long time she kept throwing up on the towel about four o'clock every morning once or twice a week. I gathered up the towel, shook it out into the plumbing, dropped it in the washing machine and put a clean towel on the bed.

I read all the health articles in my cat magazine. Recently one of the articles was about hairballs. When we next visited Dr. Coatney's office, I asked him what a hairball looks like. "Cats ingest a large amount of hair when they groom themselves," he said and described a hairball.

"Good heavens," I exclaimed. "I wonder if that is what Edith throws up every now and then."

"You groom Edith every day, don't you?"

"Oh, yes."

He asked a few more questions and suggested that perhaps Edith ought to take a lubricant and laxative in addition to the grooming. He showed me how to give it to her by putting a little of it on her upper lip, where she promptly licked it off.

"Give her about an inch of this a day," Dr. Coatney said, "in quarter-inch bites."

Edith's lubricant is brown and malt-flavored.

She soon taught me I did not need to smear it on her beautiful fur. All I need to do is squeeze a little bit of it onto my finger, and she licks it off, one quarter inch at a time. I give it at the end of our grooming session.

We do have one little problem. She wants to end the grooming sooner than she should just so she can have her lubricant. She considers it, I am sure, a great treat.

I wrote a column about the hairballs and a reader called in a nasty comment to our "Speak Up" column. He said if Roz Young didn't have any more news to write about than her cat's hair balls, she should stop writing.

I was a little mindful of that comment when I wrote again about a problem that worried me: Edith's had lost her appetite and seemed to be feeling unwell. Dr. Coatney passed his educated hands over her body, pressing here and there. At one spot she turned and growled at him.

"Ah ha!" he said. "Edith has gastritis."

"What's that?"

"Inflammation of the stomach."

"How did she get it?"

"Edith is an older cat. It comes with age. I will give her a shot and then she must take half a teaspoonful of Pepto-Bismol twice a day for a week."

I didn't have any Pepto-Bismol; I never have

had any of it. After I took Edith home, I set off for the drug store.

My goodness. There is a regular strength Pepto-Bismol, an extra-potent variety and even pills. I looked on the bottle at what it is supposed to cure. It is good for soothing relief of upset stomach, indigestion, diarrhea, heartburn or nausea.

I felt embarrassed when I handed the bottle to the woman at the checkout counter. She might think I had one of those ailments. "It's for my cat," I told her. "Do you ever sell any of this for cats?"

"Oh, sure, all the time. All the time. Dogs, too. We sell a lot of this for pets."

I felt better.

Edith is very good about taking medicine if she likes the taste. I gave up giving her pills long ago. I can poke a pill in her mouth in the approved manner and hold her mouth shut and stroke her throat, but she keeps it in her mouth and spits it out later. That's why she takes liquid medicine, and if she likes the taste, she will lick it off a spoon and I don't even have to hold her. If she doesn't like the taste, war breaks out, unceasing, never-ending war.

Edith does not like Pepto-Bismol.

Pepto-Bismol, as everybody knows, is a brilliant shade of pink. When I tried to give it to her, we had pink spots on my suit jacket and skirt, pink on the counter, pink on the kitchen floor, pink on the wall, pink on Edith's chin, but no pink in Edith's mouth. Edith laid back her ears, her eyes filled with terror, her claws came out, she howled, she fought with the strength of ten, and then she ran under the bed.

I drove back to Dr. Coatney's office, but I was so agitated I forgot it was closed for lunch. I went next door to the library while I waited. I told Ann, one of the librarians my troubles. "You can crush a pill and put it in some food she likes well. She won't know the difference," she said.

When Dr. Coatney's office opened a while later, I was there. "Edith will not take Pepto-Bismol," I told him.

"Then pills it is," he said. He disappeared into his office.

When he returned, he had a small bottle with him. "I cut these pills into four parts," he said. "I will not charge you for cutting them. Crush them and mix then with some of Edith's favorite food or even a little bit of tuna fish. Quarter of a pill twice a day for a week."

"Do the pills have any taste?" I asked.

He laughed. "I never tasted them. You can if you want to."

Back at home I crushed quarter of a pill with the bottom of a glass on a plastic cutting board and mixed the powder with a quarter can of gourmet cat food.

Edith watched every move. "I'm adding this to make you feel better," I told her. "You have gastritis."

I set the dish down for her, and she ate it with her usual gusto. Evidently the pills don't have any taste.

Edith is well again, and I have added a bottle of Pepto-Bismol to my inventory.

As I mentioned, I wrote about Edith and the Pepto-Bismol in the newspaper. Sure enough in the next "Speak Up" column the disgruntled reader called in again that if Young had nothing better to report than her cat's gastritis, she should stop writing. I felt bad again. Then in the next "Speak Up" three readers called in that they like to read about Edith's digestive problems, and I cheered up.

That same day I went to a restaurant for lunch. I was wearing a fuchsia blazer and skirt. A woman got up from a table across the room, came to our table and said out of the side of her mouth, "I see you are wearing your Pepto-Bismol suit."

Somebody suggested I ought to send a copy of the newspaper column to the makers of Pepto-Bismol. I looked on the bottle: The maker is Procter & Gamble. I sent the column to the consumer relations department.

Back came a reply from V. S. Helton:

Dear Mrs. Young:

Thank you for writing to Procter & Gamble. We enjoyed reading the article about Edith's adventure with Pepto-Bismol.

Many thoughtful customers take the time to tell us about unusual uses they've found for our products — and this is certainly unusual! We're always delighted to learn of such positive results, even though we can't encourage this product's use on pets. For obvious reasons, we have not done the extensive clinical studies we believe would be necessary for us to confidently recommend it for this use.

Still, we're glad it helped Edith and trust she continues to do well.

Thanks again for writing.

I am glad Procter & Gamble wasn't offended that Edith refused to take Pepto-Bismol.

21.

A Humbling Lesson

In a cat magazine I read a quarter-page advertisement, in red and yellow, advertising the ultimate gift for a cat. It was a toy and shoots a laser beam and makes a red spot wherever the operator aims it.

"Just press the button and watch your cat's natural instincts take over," the copy said. "All cats of all ages just love this laser mouse toy. Even the laziest cat couch potato will go crazy over this toy."

I have worried over Edith's tendency to sleep all night, all morning, and all afternoon as she ages.

I have a toy for her at the end of a string on a fishing pole, and whenever I dangle it around her, she simply lies down and rests until I get tired swinging it over her. She will bat at it once or twice if I find just the right angle to pass it over her head, but I can even let it dangle on her back, on the top of her head and even right on her nose and she will just lie there, not moving a muscle.

"I was at a cat show in New York City," said my grandson. "All the judges are using those laser toys to test cats' reactions instead of peacock feathers," he said.

What is good enough for cat judges in New York City is none too good for Edith in Ohio, I reasoned, and sent off an order.

It took a long time for the toy to arrive. I suppose thousands of cat owners had read that same advertisement and got in ahead of me.

Finally, however, it did come.

"Edith!" She came running to see what the mail had brought for her. I opened the box and fitted the batteries into the case. I shone a bright red spot on the floor in front of Edith.

She didn't even look at it.

Instead she sat up on her haunches and looked up at me, pointing the laser beam now here, now there, on the floor, across the back of the white sofa, up on the wall. I could tell by the expression on her face she was trying to figure out what had gone wrong with me.

"We will try it again after you have rested," I told her. "I am exhausted."

I tried it again later on in the day. Edith watched me shooting the laser beam all over the place and then yawned.

The laser toy that cats of all ages love was simply not for Edith. I put it back in its box and wrote the company a nice letter about how I thought that my cat was too smart to be fooled by a laser. "She thinks I have lost my marbles, throwing that laser spot all over the place," I told them. "There is nothing wrong with the toy, but I hope you will give me my money back."

They sent me a check, which was very nice of them.

My friend Carolyn received a somewhat similar electronic toy for Christmas. It was an imitation fish bowl with a pair of battery-operated fish, one blue, one red, swimming around in the water. They looked exactly like real fish, swimming in random movements, here and there, their tails and fins twisting realistically in the water. The fish look so real and their swimming pattern is so natural that you can't tell they are artificial fish.

We thought that Edith might like to have a bowl of fish to watch.

Carolyn brought the bowl to the house, and we set it up on a table. I brought Edith in and set her on the table.

She took one look at the fish and went into a hunting crouch she has not used since she moved with me to Bethany. She stalked those fish across the table top, her eyes never wavering from them, her tail switching portentously. She walked right up to the top of the bowl and sniffed.

Her interest, which had been at 100 a second before, dropped to absolute zero. Those fish did not smell real, and she would have none of the whole elaborate and highly expensive product of some electronics wizard's dream toy. We took the bowl down to the dining room for the residents to see, and every one of the human beings was fooled. They just wouldn't believe those fish weren't real until we turned the battery off. You can fool everybody who lives in our apartment, but you can't fool Edith.

I had seen advertisements for video programs for cats advertised in the pet shops, but I never bought Edith one because I thought she would not watch them. Susannah, who lives in the apartment building and who had a cat before she moved here, bought Edith one for Christmas. We put it on the television, and Edith sat entranced for fully twenty minutes, watching the birds, the fish, a two-toned rat and a few squirrels going back and forth across the screen. Her little head never moved as she watched the show. At last, however, a flock of ducks started parading back and forth across the screen. She sees real ducks all the time parading back and forth across her window, and she pays them no attention. Her interest flagged, and she went over by the television set and flopped down on the floor to rest.

About a week later I put the program on the VCR again and called Edith. She came running, but for a few moments she wasn't able to figure out why I had called her if I didn't intend to give her something to eat. Then a movement on the television screen caught her eye, and she sat down to watch the program the second time. She sat motionless before the screen for about fifteen minutes. When the ducks came on again, she left the room.

Catharine says that her cat Blackwell used to watch a golf ball soar through the air on the television screen, and when it disappeared she went around in back of the television to see where the ball went. Blackwell thought the golf ball was real. Edith knows that the rats, the birds, the hamsters on the video are not real because she never makes a the whole time the animals traipse back and cross the screen. If she thought they were she would attack. But the video is entertain- or her, and she will watch. Whether she will a third time is a question still to be answered.

from: *Mom*   to: *SUSAN*   *Season's Greetings*

22.
Elm Leaf Salad

Far off many years ago in China a nurseryman planted the seed which sprouted into an elm tree. As the little sapling began to grow in his bonsai nursery, he trained it, pruning top and roots and bending the thickening trunk with copper wire.

The tree was twenty-five years old by the time I saw it in a nursery and bought it. It stood about ten inches tall in its bonsai pot. It had 40 branches, each covered with bright green serrated leaves three-fourths of an inch long. The twisted trunk was four inches in circumference.

I brought it home from the greenhouse importer and placed it on a tray under grow lights in my bedroom.

In a few days it began to lose leaves. I found some of the leaves lying on the soil in the pot. Others lay on the carpet under the table which held the plant.

"Sometimes plants, particular woody plants, lose their leaves when they move from a humid greenhouse to the drier air of a home," one of my gardening books said. "It will take some time for them to adjust to the more arid environment of a home."

I keep each of my bonsai plants on a tray above a grid that rests on a water reservoir. Sometimes the reservoir dries out when I am not looking. I kept the reservoir under the elm tree filled and sprayed the tree daily with a mist.

Still it continued to lose leaves and soon there was nothing left of it except the trunk and the branches.

I kept it watered. I fertilized it. Every day I inspected the bare branches. Two weeks passed and I began to see little bumps growing out of the desiccated-looking branches. It was alive!

The little bumps turned into bigger bumps and finally I could see even without the magnifying glass that the little tree was in the process of getting a new coat of leaves.

In three weeks' time the tree put on a new coat and looked healthy once again.

The bonsai tray sits on the top of a shoe cabinet about four feet tall. Not far from it is a television set. One morning when I came into the room to make the bed, I was surprised to see Edith sitting on top of the television set. "What are you doing up here?" I asked. I picked her up and set her down on the floor.

She was up on the television again the next day. I found the little box on which she was sitting, which had something to do with cable television, was warm to the touch. "Oh, well," I said to myself, "she has just discovered this little warm spot and likes it."

The next morning long before rising time, a strange noise in the bedroom woke me. I glanced down at the foot of the bed. Edith was not in her customary place.

I switched on the light. Edith had jumped from the television set to the top of the shoe cabinet. There was just room for her to walk along the edge of the bonsai tray and that is what she was doing.

"Edith! No!"

She paid not the slightest attention to me but stood on the edge of the cabinet, peering at the elm tree.

I got out of bed and snatched her off the cabinet. "You must not bother the tree," I told her. "I know it is new and you have to inspect everything new in the house, but you must not get up there again." She said never a word.

The tree began to shed its leaves again.

Then one morning after breakfast I found on the beige carpet evidence that some of Edith's food had not agreed with her and she coughed it up. I put on my spectacles and inspected the heap on the carpet. It reminded me of the time Edith ate the six rubber bands all at once.

This time the heap was composed entirely of green elm leaves.

It has been years since I grew anything green for Edith to eat. I never take her out on the grass any more or walking in the cemetery because she will eat the grass and then it makes her sick. Dr. Coatney said it is too harsh for her digestive system.

I have three other bonsai, a fig tree and two carissas. Edith never has bothered them. Then I brought home the elm tree and bang! Munch, munch, munch.

I took two dry cleaning plastic bags and fashioned them into a transparent fence around the elm tree.

During the next night I heard that funny noise again. I turned on the light, and there inside the plastic bags stood Edith, having herself a small elm salad.

This time I had to go to the hardware store, buy a sheet of heavy-weight plastic, cut a length of it to go entirely around the oblong light fixture over the tree, tape the plastic on the light cover and fasten it around the bottom with a dozen spring clothes pins.

Now I have to unfasten the clothes pins every

morning to turn on the light and every evening to turn it off. Lately I have noticed that Edith watches very intently when I unfasten the pins.

I have looked up in several cat care books and found lists of 124 different plants from anemone to yew that cats have been known to eat and many of which are poisonous to them. In no list have I found elm leaves.

Edith must be the only cat in the world who has eaten the leaves off an elm tree.

23.

In Appreciation

Edith is an accommodating, patient, uncomplaining, self-reliant, polite and loving friend.

She is accommodating.

Whatever I do, she does, too. When I go to bed every night at 10:00 p. m., an hour of she chose originally, she busies herself with the last supper of the day and arrives in the bedroom at 10:10. As soon as I am comfortably arranged in bed to watch television until the 11:30 news is over, she hops up on the bed, walks to the foot takes a cursory look at the program and then settles down for the night on her towel at the foot of the bed.

I awaken at 5:00 A. M. every morning. She is still sleeping, but the moment I sit up on the side of the bed, she gets up. I walk to the door to see whether the newspaper has come, and she walks with me. If it has come, I go back to bed, turn on the reading light and scan the news of the day. She jumps back up on the bed, settles down on my outstretched legs and snoozes there until the clock radio stirs to life at 6:00. When I get up for the second time, she waits until I put on my house coat and walks in front of me to the kitchen. I give her breakfast, which she consumes before the water for my coffee has boiled.

In the daytime if I am working at the computer, she takes a nap on the other office chair. If I sit on the sofa to read, she takes a nap on the sofa beside me. If I watch television in the evening, and I will say she disapproves of the habit, she does not object but climbs to the top of her tree and supervises activities in the world outside her window until bedtime, whereupon she lets me know it is time to go to bed.

Edith is patient.

When she wants something, she will sit motionless for ages, her unblinking green eyes staring up at me until I look up from my book or my plate and ask her what she wants. She never meows or scratches; she waits and waits and waits. Her patience makes me feel ashamed of myself for making her wait. If I am hopelessly buried in a book and fail to see her, she sometimes gives up and goes off to take a nap until I have finished reading.

She does not complain.

She gets only one ounce of dry food a day and

one ounce of meat a day, doled out in many small meals. Sometimes there are only six little bits of dry food left at the end of the day, but no matter how small the amount I put into her bowl, she accepts it as if it were the most sumptuous banquet.

When she is not feeling well, she says never a word, but suffers silently until I notice she is unwell. Sometimes she picks up a virus or an infection, but she lets her doctor give her shots and takes her medicine as if it just what cats like best.

She is self-reliant.

She plays now and then with a small toy someone has given her and keeps a constant eye through the windows, looking for squirrels or wandering cats. She climbs her tree and surveys the garden and the lake, looking for trespassers. The innocent stroller walking by never knows that just inside our window a crouches a jungle guard who watches every step with piercing gaze and switching tail. She fills in the rest of her day with naps, her chin resting on her paw.

Edith is polite.

She likes guests to visit, and she welcomes them warmly when they arrive. If they stay, however, beyond 9:00 p. m., she thinks it is time for them to go home. She is too mannerly to tell them so by staring at them and meowing, but she plods through the living room with a purposeful look on her face and goes to the door and sits down to wait. Most of the guests know when it is time to go, but if some linger, she makes another sally through the room, going to the back door and looking purposefully out and returning to the hall door where she knows they will leave, sits down and waits and waits and waits.

When they do leave, she walks out into the hall and waits until they disappear into the elevator. Then she goes back into the kitchen for the snack she knows will appear.

Edith is loving.

When I wash my face in the morning, she waits by the bathroom door. One morning I said to her, "Edith, would you like your face washed?" She washes her own face by wetting a paw and rubbing it over her face and behind her ears, but it can't be a good or satisfying wash. I took a washcloth, held it under the hot water faucet, wrung it out and made it into a nice, warm packet. I held it out for her inspection and then rubbed it over her forehead, her cheeks, her mouth, and behind her ears with little, short strokes such as her mother probably gave her when she was a kitten. I even bought her a special wash cloth with a nubby surface like her mother's tongue. Since that first time, she comes every morning to have her face washed. I am delighted to do this for her.

Edith is not so spry now as she once was. It is

hard for her to jump up on the chest to be groomed and onto the bed for her nap. Sometimes she tries but isn't able to make the jump. Dr. Coatney says, "I think it is because of her age." She has arthritis.

I am not as agile as I would like to be, either. Edith and I are growing older together. It makes me happy to have such a companionable, patient, uncomplaining, self-reliant, polite and loving friend, and I try to make her happy, too. I am thankful every day that she came to live with me. Every night when I turn out the light and feel her warm and solid body stretched out at the foot of the bed, I am content and drift off joyfully to sleep. Every morning when I wake and see her stretched out on her side, her soft side rising and falling with her breath, I arise with joy.

Another day has come for us to be happy together.

Resources

Books

Browning, Robert. *Complete Works*, Athens, Ohio University Press, 1969.

Evans, J. M. and White, Kay. *Catlopedia: A Complete Guide to Cat Care*. New York: Howell Book House, 1997.

Gaskell, Elizabeth, *Cranford*. London: Dent, 1966, c. 1906.

The Hymnal 1982. New York: The Church Hymnal Corporation, 1985.

The New Encyclopedia Britannica. Chicago: Encyclopedia Britannica, Inc., 1994.

The Oxford English Dictionary. Oxford and New York, The Oxford University Press, 1989.

Oxford Dictionary of Christian Names. London, Oxford University Press, 1977.

Roman Ritual Book of Blessings. New York, Catholic Book Publishing Co., 1989.

Shojai, Amy D. *The Purina Encyclopedia of Cat Care*. New York: Ballantine Books, 1998.

Siegal, Mordecai, editor, *The Cornell Book of Cats*. New York, Villard Books, 1997.

This Fabulous Century. "Death of Floyd Collins." New York:

Time-Life Books, vol. III, 1969.

Letter

Wilbourn, Carole C. New York, 1990

About the Author

Edith & Roz

Rosamond M. Young (Roz) and Edith live in Dayton, Ohio, where Roz writes a weekly column for the local newspaper, and Edith minds her own business, which tends to be enjoying herself as much as possible. Although a senior cat now, Edith still manages to inject a bit of chaos into Roz's daily routine whenever possible.